PROTECTING
NETWORK SECURITY
WITH PYTHON AND SCAPY

A GUIDE TO DETECTING VULNERABILITIES AND AUTOMATING
NETWORK SECURITY

IAN EBERT

Disclaimer

The content presented in this book is for educational and informational purposes only. Every effort has been made to ensure the accuracy of the information at the time of publication; however, the author(s) and publisher make no representations or warranties about the completeness, accuracy, or current applicability of the material provided.

This book may include references to software, hardware, systems, or processes that are subject to change over time. Readers are encouraged to verify the information and ensure compatibility with their specific setups or environments before implementing any of the recommendations, instructions, or code snippets presented. Individual results may vary based on varying hardware, software versions, and user expertise.

The author(s) and publisher assume no liability for any errors, omissions, or outcomes that may arise from the application or use of the information in this book. The implementation of any techniques, processes, or configurations described herein is solely at the reader's own risk. It is recommended that users back up their data and systems and take necessary precautions before making any changes.

For complex technical challenges or if uncertainty arises, consulting with a qualified professional or technical expert is advisable.

Contents

Chapter 1: Introduction to Network Security

Overview of Network Security Principles

Network security encompasses the policies, practices, and technologies designed to protect networks, devices, and data from unauthorized access, attacks, and damage. At its core, network security aims to maintain the confidentiality, integrity, and availability of information. This triad—often referred to as the CIA triad—is fundamental to understanding how security measures are implemented and evaluated.

Confidentiality refers to ensuring that sensitive information is accessible only to those who are authorized to view it. Techniques to maintain confidentiality include encryption, access control mechanisms, and secure communication protocols. For instance, when data is transmitted over the internet, it can be encrypted using protocols such as HTTPS or VPNs to prevent unauthorized interception.

Integrity involves ensuring that data remains accurate and unaltered during transmission or storage. Integrity is often maintained through checksums, hashes, and digital signatures, which verify that data has not been tampered with. For example, when software is downloaded, its integrity can be verified by checking its hash against a known value.

Availability ensures that authorized users have reliable access to resources and information when needed. Availability can be threatened by various factors, including hardware failures, natural disasters, and denial-of-service attacks. Measures to enhance availability include redundant systems, failover mechanisms, and robust backup strategies.

Effective network security requires a multi-layered approach. Organizations typically implement several strategies to protect their networks, including firewalls, intrusion detection systems (IDS), intrusion prevention systems (IPS), and antivirus software. Firewalls act as barriers between trusted internal networks and untrusted external networks, controlling incoming and outgoing traffic based on predetermined security rules. IDS and IPS monitor network traffic for suspicious activity and can take action to mitigate threats.

Another critical aspect of network security is the human element. Employees and users play a significant role in maintaining security. Social engineering attacks, such as phishing, exploit human vulnerabilities to gain unauthorized access to systems. Therefore, organizations must invest in user education and awareness programs to promote safe computing practices and to recognize potential threats.

Finally, network security is a dynamic field that must evolve with the ever-changing landscape of threats. New vulnerabilities and attack vectors continually emerge, driven by advancements in technology and shifts in user behavior. Organizations must adopt a proactive stance, regularly updating their security policies, tools, and practices to defend against these evolving threats.

Importance of Proactive Security Measures

In today's digital landscape, cyber threats are ubiquitous and increasingly sophisticated. The importance of proactive security measures cannot be overstated. Rather than waiting for an attack to occur and reacting to it, organizations must adopt a forward-thinking approach to safeguard their networks.

Proactive security measures involve identifying potential vulnerabilities and implementing solutions to mitigate them before they can be exploited. This approach includes regular risk assessments, vulnerability scanning, and penetration testing to uncover weaknesses in network defenses. By discovering and addressing vulnerabilities proactively, organizations can significantly reduce the risk of successful attacks.

Additionally, proactive security measures encompass the establishment of robust security policies and procedures. These policies guide employees on acceptable use, data protection, and incident response. Clear guidelines help create a security-conscious culture within an organization, reducing the likelihood of human errors that could lead to breaches.

Investing in security technology is another critical component of a proactive strategy. Firewalls, IDS/IPS, antivirus software, and endpoint detection and response (EDR) tools work together to create a robust security posture. Regular updates and patches to software and systems are also essential to protect against newly discovered vulnerabilities.

Another vital aspect of proactive security is the implementation of monitoring and logging. Continuous monitoring of network traffic allows organizations to detect unusual patterns that may indicate a breach or an attempted attack. Logs provide a historical record of network activity, aiding in forensic investigations and compliance with regulatory requirements.

Moreover, organizations should engage in threat intelligence gathering, which involves collecting and analyzing information about current and emerging threats. By staying informed about the latest attack vectors and trends, organizations can adjust their security strategies to address specific threats relevant to their environment.

Finally, proactive security measures contribute to building trust with clients, partners, and stakeholders. In an era where data breaches can result in significant financial losses and reputational damage, demonstrating a commitment to cybersecurity can enhance an organization's credibility and competitiveness.

Introduction to Python and Scapy

As the demand for robust network security solutions grows, so does the need for effective tools to analyze and protect networks. Python, a versatile and powerful programming language, has gained significant traction in the cybersecurity community. Its simplicity, readability, and extensive library support make it an ideal choice for developing security tools and automating tasks.

One of the most notable libraries in Python for network analysis is Scapy. Scapy is a powerful interactive packet manipulation tool that allows users to create, send, and analyze network packets. It supports a wide variety of protocols and provides a user-friendly interface for network analysis, making it a favorite among security professionals and researchers.

Scapy's capabilities extend beyond simple packet sniffing. Users can craft custom packets, perform network scans, and even implement protocols. This flexibility makes Scapy a valuable asset for vulnerability assessment, penetration testing, and network forensics.

For example, Scapy can be used to conduct ARP spoofing attacks, where an attacker impersonates another device on the network to intercept traffic. Conversely, it can also be employed to create countermeasures against such attacks by monitoring for suspicious ARP activity.

Moreover, Scapy allows users to automate repetitive tasks, streamlining security assessments and analysis. By scripting security workflows in Python, professionals can save time and ensure consistency in their assessments. This automation can include regular vulnerability scans, data collection for analysis, and even incident response actions.

The integration of Python and Scapy into network security practices represents a shift toward more dynamic and adaptable approaches to cybersecurity. As threats evolve, so too must the tools used to combat them. With its open-source nature and active community, Scapy continues to evolve, offering new features and capabilities to meet the needs of security practitioners.

In summary, the integration of proactive security measures with the capabilities of Python and Scapy provides a powerful framework for enhancing network security. By understanding and applying the principles of network security, organizations can better protect their assets, respond to threats, and maintain the integrity of their networks.

Chapter 2: Setting Up Your Environment

Installing Python and Scapy

To begin working in the field of network security using Python and Scapy, the first step is setting up your development environment. This involves installing Python and the Scapy library, which will allow you to execute various network security tasks effectively. Python is a widely used programming language that supports multiple platforms, and Scapy is a powerful tool that simplifies packet manipulation and analysis.

Installing Python

Download Python: The first step is to download the latest version of Python from the official website, python.org. It is recommended to use Python 3, as Python 2 is no longer supported and lacks several features and libraries that are essential for current development.

Run the Installer: After downloading, run the installer. On Windows, ensure to check the option "Add Python to PATH" during installation. This step is crucial, as it allows you to execute Python commands from the command line or terminal without specifying the full path.

Verify the Installation: After the installation is complete, you can verify that Python has been successfully installed by opening a command prompt (Windows) or terminal (macOS/Linux) and typing:
bash

Copy code

```
python --version
```

or for some systems:
bash

Copy code

```
python3 --version
```

This command should return the version of Python you installed.

Installing Scapy

Using pip: Scapy can be easily installed using `pip`, Python's package manager. To install Scapy, open a command prompt or terminal and execute the following command:
bash

Copy code

```
pip install scapy
```

If you are using Python 3, you may need to use `pip3` instead:

bash
Copy code
```
pip3 install scapy
```

Verify Scapy Installation: After the installation, you can verify that Scapy has been installed correctly by launching a Python interactive shell. Type:
python
Copy code
```
import scapy
print(scapy.__version__)
```

This should return the version number of Scapy you have installed, confirming that it is ready for use.

Dependencies: Scapy may require additional libraries depending on your operating system. For instance, on Windows, you might need to install WinPcap or Npcap to enable packet capture functionality. On macOS and Linux, ensure that you have the necessary permissions to capture packets, which often involves running scripts with root or administrator privileges.

Configuring Necessary Libraries and Dependencies

After installing Python and Scapy, it is crucial to ensure that your environment is configured correctly to enable seamless operation. This section will discuss configuring dependencies, libraries, and network permissions that may be necessary for Scapy to function effectively.

Installing Additional Libraries

Scapy leverages several Python libraries that may need to be installed separately. Common libraries that are often used with Scapy include:

NumPy: This library is essential for efficient numerical calculations and array operations. You can install it using:
bash
Copy code

```
pip install numpy
```

Matplotlib: If you plan to visualize network data or packet information, Matplotlib is a useful library for creating plots and graphs. Install it using:
bash
Copy code

```
pip install matplotlib
```

Pandas: For handling and analyzing structured data, Pandas can be a valuable addition to your toolkit. It can be installed with:

bash

Copy code

```
pip install pandas
```

Configuring Network Permissions

To effectively utilize Scapy, you must ensure that you have the appropriate permissions to capture and manipulate network packets. On different operating systems, this may involve various steps:

Windows: If you're using Windows, ensure that you have installed either WinPcap or Npcap. These drivers enable packet capturing in Scapy. During the installation of Npcap, make sure to select the option for "WinPcap API-compatible mode," which allows Scapy to function correctly.

Linux: On Linux, capturing packets typically requires root privileges. You can run your Python scripts with sudo to grant the necessary permissions. For instance:

bash

Copy code

```
sudo python3 your_script.py
```

macOS: Similar to Linux, macOS also requires elevated privileges to capture packets. Running your script with `sudo` will be necessary. Additionally, ensure that you have the necessary permissions to access the network interfaces.

Setting Up a Virtual Environment

Using a virtual environment for your Python projects is highly recommended, as it helps manage dependencies and prevents conflicts between different projects. A virtual environment allows you to create isolated environments for each of your Python projects.

Creating a Virtual Environment: You can create a virtual environment using the following command:
bash
Copy code

```
python -m venv myenv
```

Replace `myenv` with the desired name of your environment.
Activating the Virtual Environment:

On Windows:
bash
Copy code

```
myenv\Scripts\activate
```

On macOS/Linux:
bash
Copy code

```
source myenv/bin/activate
```

Installing Scapy in the Virtual Environment: Once the virtual environment is activated, any packages you install using `pip` will be contained within that environment. Therefore, install Scapy and any other necessary libraries after activating your virtual environment.

Deactivating the Virtual Environment: To exit the virtual environment, simply type:
bash
Copy code

```
deactivate
```

By using a virtual environment, you ensure that your main Python installation remains clean and that different projects can use different library versions without conflict.

Setting Up a Development Environment

Creating an efficient development environment can significantly enhance your productivity as you work with Python and Scapy. Here are some essential components and tools that you should consider incorporating into your setup:

Integrated Development Environment (IDE)

Choosing the right IDE can streamline your coding process. Popular choices for Python development include:

PyCharm: A powerful IDE specifically designed for Python development. It offers features such as code completion, debugging tools, and integrated version control. The Community Edition is free and sufficient for most users.

Visual Studio Code: A lightweight and highly customizable editor that supports various programming languages, including Python. With the right extensions, it can provide many features of a full IDE.

Jupyter Notebook: If you prefer an interactive coding environment, Jupyter Notebook allows you to write and execute Python code in a web-based format. It's particularly useful for data analysis and visualization tasks.

Version Control System

Using a version control system, such as Git, is crucial for managing changes to your code. It allows you to track modifications, collaborate with others, and revert to previous versions if needed. Setting up a Git repository for your project is straightforward:

Initialize a Git Repository: Inside your project directory, run:
bash
Copy code
```
git init
```

Add Files to the Repository: You can stage files for commit with:
bash
Copy code
```
git add .
```

Commit Your Changes: To save your changes, execute:
bash

Copy code
```
git commit -m "Initial commit"
```

Using a Remote Repository: If you want to collaborate with others, consider using platforms like GitHub, GitLab, or Bitbucket to host your remote repositories. This way, you can easily share your work and contribute to projects.

Documentation and Learning Resources

Effective documentation is key to understanding and maintaining your code. Make it a habit to document your functions and modules thoroughly. You can use docstrings in Python to explain what your code does, its parameters, and return values. For example:

python
Copy code
```
def calculate_sum(a, b):
    " " "

Calculate the sum of two numbers.

Parameters:
a (int or float): The first number.
b (int or float): The second number.
```

```
Returns:
int or float: The sum of a and b.
" " "

return a + b
```

Additionally, consider using tools like Sphinx or MkDocs to generate documentation for your projects automatically.

Exploring Online Resources

The Python and Scapy communities are vibrant and active, providing a wealth of online resources. Some valuable platforms include:

Official Documentation: The Python Documentation and Scapy Documentation are invaluable resources for learning about language features and library functions.

Forums and Communities: Websites like Stack Overflow and Reddit's r/netsec provide platforms for asking questions, sharing knowledge, and connecting with other cybersecurity enthusiasts.

Tutorials and Courses: Consider enrolling in online courses focused on Python for cybersecurity. Platforms like Coursera, Udemy, and Pluralsight offer a variety of courses catering to different skill levels.

In summary, setting up your environment for network security tasks using Python and Scapy involves installing Python, configuring necessary libraries, setting up a virtual environment, and creating an efficient development workflow. By following these steps, you will be well-equipped to start exploring and leveraging the capabilities of Python and Scapy in your network security endeavors.

Chapter 3: Understanding Network Protocols

Overview of Common Network Protocols

Network protocols are essential rules and standards that dictate how data is transmitted and received across networks. They ensure communication between devices, allowing for the orderly exchange of information. Understanding these protocols is critical for anyone working in network security, as vulnerabilities can often be traced back to how these protocols operate or are implemented.

TCP/IP (Transmission Control Protocol/Internet Protocol)

TCP/IP is the foundational protocol suite for the internet and most modern networks. It consists of two main layers: the Internet Protocol (IP) and the Transmission Control Protocol (TCP).

Internet Protocol (IP): Responsible for addressing and routing packets of data across networks. Each device on a network is assigned a unique IP address, which serves as its identifier. IP operates at the Network Layer of the OSI (Open Systems Interconnection) model. There are two versions of IP currently in use: IPv4 and IPv6. IPv4, which uses 32-bit addresses, is limited to approximately 4.3 billion unique addresses. IPv6, introduced to address the limitations of IPv4, uses 128-bit addresses, allowing for a virtually limitless number of unique addresses.

Transmission Control Protocol (TCP): This protocol operates at the Transport Layer and is responsible for ensuring reliable communication between devices. TCP establishes a connection before data transfer, providing error-checking and ensuring that data packets are delivered in the correct order. If packets are lost or corrupted during transmission, TCP can request retransmission, ensuring data integrity.

Together, TCP and IP form the backbone of the internet, enabling diverse applications such as web browsing, email, and file transfers.

UDP (User Datagram Protocol)

UDP is another transport layer protocol, often contrasted with TCP. While TCP provides reliable, ordered communication, UDP is a connectionless protocol that prioritizes speed over reliability. It does not establish a connection before sending data, nor does it guarantee packet delivery or order.

Characteristics of UDP: Because of its lightweight nature, UDP is ideal for applications where speed is critical and occasional data loss is acceptable. Examples include live video streaming, online gaming, and voice over IP (VoIP) communications. However, the lack of reliability means that applications using UDP must implement their own error-checking and recovery mechanisms if needed.

ICMP (Internet Control Message Protocol)

ICMP is a network layer protocol used for diagnostic and control purposes. It facilitates error reporting and management of network devices. One of the most common uses of ICMP is the "ping" command, which sends echo request messages to a target device and listens for echo replies.

Functions of ICMP: ICMP messages can indicate network conditions such as unreachable hosts, time exceeded for packet delivery, or route redirection. However, ICMP can also be exploited in attacks, such as ping floods or ICMP tunneling, making it crucial to monitor and manage ICMP traffic in network security.

HTTP/HTTPS (Hypertext Transfer Protocol/Secure)

HTTP is the protocol used for transferring hypertext documents on the World Wide Web. It operates at the application layer and follows a request-response model where clients (web browsers) send requests to servers, which respond with requested resources.

HTTPS: The secure version of HTTP, HTTPS encrypts data transmitted between clients and servers using protocols such as SSL (Secure Sockets Layer) or TLS (Transport Layer Security). This encryption ensures the confidentiality and integrity of data, protecting against eavesdropping and tampering. Understanding HTTP and HTTPS is vital for securing web applications and identifying potential vulnerabilities, such as SSL/TLS misconfigurations.

FTP (File Transfer Protocol)

FTP is a standard network protocol used for transferring files between a client and a server. It operates at the application layer and supports both anonymous and authenticated access.

Security Considerations: Traditional FTP transmits data in plaintext, making it susceptible to interception. As a result, secure versions of FTP, such as FTPS (FTP Secure) and SFTP (SSH File Transfer Protocol), have been developed to encrypt data during transfer. Network security practitioners must be aware of the risks associated with unencrypted file transfers and ensure that secure methods are implemented when sensitive data is involved.

SMTP (Simple Mail Transfer Protocol)

SMTP is the protocol used for sending emails across networks. It operates at the application layer and defines the process for routing and delivering email messages between servers.

Email Security: While SMTP is effective for sending emails, it does not inherently provide security features. Techniques such as STARTTLS and SMTPS can be employed to add encryption and enhance security. Additionally, understanding email protocols is crucial for mitigating threats such as phishing, spam, and email spoofing.

How Protocols are Used in Network Security

Network protocols play a pivotal role in the design and implementation of security measures. By understanding how these protocols function, security professionals can better identify vulnerabilities and devise appropriate defenses. Here are some key considerations regarding the intersection of protocols and network security:

Protocol Vulnerabilities

Every protocol has inherent weaknesses that can be exploited by attackers. For instance, TCP's reliance on connection establishment and teardown can lead to SYN flood attacks, where an attacker sends a barrage of SYN requests without completing the handshake, overwhelming the server's resources. Similarly, UDP's lack of connection establishment makes it susceptible to reflection attacks, where an attacker sends requests to multiple servers, with the response directed to a victim's address.

Security professionals must continuously analyze protocol behaviors to identify potential vulnerabilities and implement measures to mitigate these risks. This often involves employing security mechanisms such as rate limiting, packet filtering, and intrusion detection systems.

Authentication and Encryption

Many network protocols incorporate authentication and encryption to enhance security. For instance, SSH (Secure Shell) is a protocol that provides secure remote access to servers. It encrypts data transmitted over the network and authenticates users through keys or passwords. Similarly, protocols like HTTPS utilize SSL/TLS to secure web traffic.

31

Implementing these secure protocols is crucial for protecting sensitive data during transmission. Security practitioners should prioritize the use of encrypted protocols whenever feasible and ensure proper configurations to prevent common pitfalls, such as outdated encryption algorithms.

Firewalls and Protocol Filtering

Firewalls are essential security devices that monitor and control network traffic based on predetermined security rules. They operate at various layers of the OSI model and can filter traffic based on protocols, IP addresses, ports, and other parameters.

Understanding protocols allows security teams to configure firewalls effectively. For example, a firewall can be set to allow only specific types of traffic, such as HTTP and HTTPS, while blocking all other protocols. This principle of least privilege helps minimize the attack surface and protects the network from unauthorized access.

Intrusion Detection and Prevention Systems (IDS/IPS)

IDS and IPS are security solutions designed to monitor network traffic for suspicious activity and potential threats. These systems rely on a deep understanding of protocols to detect anomalies and respond to incidents.

For instance, an IDS may analyze traffic patterns and flag unusual spikes in TCP or UDP traffic, potentially indicating a denial-of-service attack. An IPS can take proactive measures, such as dropping malicious packets or blocking specific IP addresses based on predefined rules.

Incident Response and Forensics

When security incidents occur, understanding network protocols becomes critical for incident response and forensic investigations. Analysts often need to analyze packet captures (PCAPs) to reconstruct events leading to a breach. Tools like Scapy can be employed to analyze packet data and extract relevant information, such as source and destination IP addresses, protocols used, and payload content.

Forensic investigations may involve examining logs from firewalls, IDS/IPS, and servers to identify patterns and trace the actions of attackers. Knowledge of protocols is vital for interpreting these logs and understanding how an attack unfolded.

Introduction to Packet Structure and Analysis

At the heart of network communication lies the concept of packets. Data transmitted over networks is divided into packets, each containing specific information about its origin, destination, and content. Understanding packet structure is fundamental for anyone involved in network security.

Packet Structure

A packet typically consists of two main components: the header and the payload.

Header: The header contains metadata about the packet, including source and destination IP addresses, protocol information, and control flags. The exact structure of the header varies depending on the protocol being used. For instance, an IP header contains fields such as version, header length, total length, protocol type, and checksum. Similarly, TCP and UDP headers contain source and destination port numbers, sequence numbers, and flags indicating the state of the connection.

Payload: The payload is the actual data being transmitted, which can vary in size depending on the application and protocol. For example, an HTTP packet may contain the content of a webpage, while a DNS packet might carry a query for domain name resolution.

Analyzing Packets with Scapy

Scapy provides a powerful framework for analyzing packets in Python. With Scapy, you can capture live traffic, dissect packet structures, and even craft custom packets for testing purposes.

Capturing Packets

To capture packets, Scapy uses the sniff function, which allows you to specify filters based on protocols, ports, and other criteria. For instance, to capture only HTTP traffic, you might use:

python
Copy code

```
from scapy.all import sniff

def packet_callback(packet):
print(packet.summary())

sniff(filter="tcp      port      80",
prn=packet_callback, count=10)
```

This code captures ten packets of TCP traffic on port 80 and prints a summary of each packet.

Dissecting Packets

Once packets are captured, Scapy allows you to dissect them and extract relevant information. For example, to analyze an individual packet, you can use the show method:

```python
Copy code
packet = sniff(count=1)[0]   # Capture
one packet
packet.show()      #  Display  packet
details
```

The show method provides a comprehensive breakdown of the packet's header and payload, allowing you to inspect its structure and contents.

Chapter 4: Networking Basics

Understanding Networking Fundamentals

Before diving deeper into network security, it's essential to grasp the fundamental concepts of networking. Networking involves connecting computers and devices to share resources, exchange data, and facilitate communication. This chapter will cover key networking concepts, including network topologies, protocols, devices, and addressing schemes.

Network Topologies

Network topology refers to the arrangement of various elements (links, nodes, etc.) in a computer network. Understanding different topologies is crucial for designing secure and efficient networks. Here are some common topologies:

Star Topology: In a star topology, all devices are connected to a central hub or switch. This design simplifies troubleshooting and network management. If one device fails, it doesn't affect the others, but if the central hub fails, the entire network goes down. Star topologies are widely used in local area networks (LANs).

Bus Topology: In a bus topology, all devices share a single communication line or cable. Each device is connected to the bus, allowing data to travel in both directions. This topology is inexpensive and easy to set up but can suffer from performance issues as more devices are added. A failure in the bus can disrupt communication for all devices.

Ring Topology: In a ring topology, devices are connected in a circular fashion, with each device connected to two others. Data travels in one direction around the ring. This design can provide predictable performance but is susceptible to failure; if one device fails, it can break the loop and disrupt the entire network.

Mesh Topology: A mesh topology involves multiple connections between devices, providing redundancy and reliability. In a full mesh, every device is connected to every other device. This topology is robust but can be costly and complex to set up. It's often used in critical networks where uptime is crucial.

Hybrid Topology: Many networks utilize a combination of different topologies to leverage the advantages of each. For instance, a star-bus topology combines elements of both star and bus topologies, providing flexibility and scalability.

Networking Protocols

Networking protocols are the rules and conventions for communication between network devices. Familiarity with these protocols is essential for understanding how data is transmitted and received. Some common networking protocols include:

TCP/IP: As discussed in the previous chapter, TCP/IP is the foundational protocol suite for the internet. It enables reliable communication and data exchange across diverse networks.

HTTP/HTTPS: These protocols are used for transferring web pages and other resources over the internet. HTTPS includes security measures to protect data during transmission.

FTP: This protocol facilitates file transfer between clients and servers, allowing for both upload and download functionalities.

DNS (Domain Name System): DNS translates human-readable domain names (like www.example.com) into IP addresses. This process is crucial for routing traffic across the internet.

DHCP (Dynamic Host Configuration Protocol): DHCP automatically assigns IP addresses and other network configuration settings to devices on a network, simplifying the management of IP address allocation.

Networking Devices

Various devices are integral to the functioning of networks. Understanding these devices and their roles is crucial for network security professionals. Key networking devices include:

Router: A router connects multiple networks and routes data between them. It uses IP addresses to determine the best path for data packets. Routers also often include security features, such as firewalls, to protect the networks they connect.

Switch: A switch operates at the data link layer and connects devices within the same network. It uses MAC addresses to forward data to the correct destination. Switches improve network efficiency by reducing collisions and allowing simultaneous data transmissions.

Firewall: A firewall monitors and controls incoming and outgoing network traffic based on predetermined security rules. It serves as a barrier between trusted and untrusted networks, preventing unauthorized access.

Access Point (AP): An access point allows wireless devices to connect to a wired network. It acts as a bridge between wireless clients and the wired infrastructure, facilitating wireless communication.

Modem: A modem modulates and demodulates signals for data transmission over telephone lines or cable systems. It connects a network to the internet and converts digital data from a computer into a format suitable for transmission over these lines.

Addressing Schemes

Understanding addressing schemes is fundamental to networking. Every device on a network requires a unique identifier to facilitate communication. Key addressing concepts include:

IP Addressing: An IP address is a unique numerical label assigned to each device connected to a network. There are two versions of IP addressing: IPv4 and IPv6. IPv4 addresses are 32 bits long and written in decimal format (e.g., 192.168.1.1), while IPv6 addresses are 128 bits long and written in hexadecimal format (e.g., 2001:0db8:85a3:0000:0000:8a2e:0370:7334).

Subnetting: Subnetting is the practice of dividing a larger network into smaller, manageable subnetworks (subnets). This enhances network performance and security by limiting broadcast traffic and segmenting network traffic.

MAC Addressing: A MAC address (Media Access Control address) is a unique identifier assigned to network interfaces for communications at the data link layer. MAC addresses are used within local networks to facilitate data transfer between devices.

The OSI Model

The OSI (Open Systems Interconnection) model is a conceptual framework used to understand network interactions in seven layers. Each layer serves a specific function in the communication process:

Physical Layer: This layer deals with the physical transmission of data over network media, such as cables, switches, and wireless signals.

Data Link Layer: This layer provides node-to-node data transfer and error detection/correction. It encapsulates data into frames for transmission.

Network Layer: The network layer manages routing and forwarding of data packets. It handles addressing, such as IP addressing, and determines the best path for data transmission.

Transport Layer: This layer ensures reliable data transfer between devices, managing error recovery, flow control, and segmentation of data into packets. Protocols like TCP and UDP operate at this layer.

Session Layer: The session layer manages sessions or connections between applications, establishing, maintaining, and terminating connections as needed.

Presentation Layer: This layer formats and encrypts data for the application layer. It ensures that data is presented in a readable format, handling data translation, compression, and encryption.

Application Layer: The topmost layer, the application layer, provides network services directly to user applications. Protocols like HTTP, FTP, and SMTP operate at this layer, enabling various services and communication functionalities.

Understanding the OSI model is vital for diagnosing network issues and implementing security measures, as it helps identify the layer where problems or vulnerabilities may arise.

Common Networking Scenarios

A solid grasp of common networking scenarios can help security professionals understand potential vulnerabilities and design appropriate defenses. Some typical scenarios include:

Local Area Network (LAN)

A LAN connects devices within a limited geographical area, such as a home, office, or school. LANs facilitate resource sharing, including files, printers, and internet access. Understanding LAN design, topology, and security configurations is crucial for protecting sensitive data and ensuring reliable communication.

Wide Area Network (WAN)

A WAN connects devices across broader geographical areas, often using leased telecommunication lines. The internet is the largest example of a WAN. Security considerations for WANs include protecting data transmitted over public networks and ensuring secure remote access.

Virtual Private Network (VPN)

A VPN creates a secure, encrypted connection over a less secure network, such as the internet. It allows users to send and receive data as if their devices were directly connected to a private network. Understanding VPN technology and its security implications is essential for protecting remote access and ensuring data confidentiality.

Wireless Networks

Wireless networks facilitate connectivity without physical cabling. While convenient, they also present unique security challenges, such as unauthorized access and eavesdropping. Implementing security measures like WPA3 encryption, strong passwords, and regular monitoring is vital for protecting wireless networks.

Network Attacks and Threats

Familiarity with common network attacks is essential for understanding how to secure networks. Some prevalent threats include:

Denial of Service (DoS) Attacks: These attacks overwhelm a target with excessive traffic, rendering it inaccessible. Understanding how to mitigate DoS attacks, such as through rate limiting and firewalls, is crucial for maintaining availability.

Man-in-the-Middle (MitM) Attacks: In MitM attacks, an attacker intercepts and potentially alters communication between two parties. Using encryption and secure protocols is essential to defend against such attacks.

Phishing: Phishing attacks manipulate users into providing sensitive information by impersonating legitimate entities. User education and awareness are vital for reducing the risk of falling victim to phishing attempts.

Summary of Networking Basics

Networking fundamentals are critical for understanding how data is transmitted, received, and secured across networks. By grasping the principles of network topologies, protocols, devices, addressing schemes, and common scenarios, security professionals can design and implement effective security measures. This foundational knowledge serves as a stepping stone for delving deeper into specific network security practices and tools. Understanding the intricacies of networking enhances the ability to identify vulnerabilities, analyze security incidents, and devise proactive strategies to protect valuable assets in a continuously evolving digital landscape.

Chapter 5: Introduction to Python and Scapy

Introduction to Python Programming

Python is a versatile, high-level programming language known for its simplicity and readability, making it an ideal choice for both beginners and experienced developers. Its extensive libraries and frameworks enable rapid development across various domains, including web development, data analysis, artificial intelligence, and, notably, network security.

Features of Python

Python boasts several features that contribute to its popularity:

Readability and Simplicity: Python's syntax is clear and intuitive, allowing developers to write code that is easy to understand. This reduces the learning curve and enhances collaboration among developers.

Extensive Libraries: Python has a vast standard library and a rich ecosystem of third-party libraries that simplify tasks ranging from data manipulation to web scraping. Libraries such as NumPy and Pandas are essential for data analysis, while Flask and Django are popular for web development.

Cross-Platform Compatibility: Python runs on various operating systems, including Windows, macOS, and Linux. This makes it suitable for developing applications that need to function across different environments.

Community Support: Python has a large and active community, providing a wealth of resources, tutorials, and documentation. This support network makes it easier for developers to find solutions to common problems.

Setting Up the Python Environment

To start using Python for network security tasks, it is essential to set up the development environment. This includes installing Python, configuring the Integrated Development Environment (IDE), and managing packages.

Installing Python: The first step is to download and install Python from the official website (python.org). The latest version is recommended to ensure access to the newest features and security updates.

Choosing an IDE: While Python can be written in any text editor, using an IDE can enhance productivity. Popular choices include PyCharm, Visual Studio Code, and Jupyter Notebook. These IDEs provide features such as syntax highlighting, debugging tools, and code completion.

Managing Packages with pip: Python's package manager, pip, allows developers to install and manage third-party libraries easily. For example, to install Scapy, you can run the following command in the terminal:

bash

Copy code

```
pip install scapy
```

Python for Network Security

Python's versatility makes it particularly well-suited for network security tasks. Security professionals can leverage Python to automate repetitive tasks, analyze network traffic, and develop custom security tools. Its ability to handle various data formats, interact with APIs, and integrate with other tools enhances its utility in the cybersecurity domain.

Introduction to Scapy

Scapy is a powerful Python library designed for packet manipulation and network traffic analysis. It allows users to create, send, and receive packets, making it an invaluable tool for network security professionals. Scapy's flexibility and ease of use enable a wide range of applications, from simple packet crafting to advanced network reconnaissance.

Key Features of Scapy

Scapy offers several features that distinguish it from other packet manipulation tools:

Packet Crafting: Scapy allows users to create custom packets at various layers of the OSI model. This capability enables testing and simulating different network scenarios, such as denial-of-service attacks or intrusion detection.

Packet Sniffing: Scapy can capture live network traffic, allowing users to analyze packet flows in real time. This feature is useful for monitoring network activity, detecting anomalies, and troubleshooting issues.

Protocol Support: Scapy supports a wide range of network protocols, including TCP, UDP, ICMP, ARP, DNS, and more. This extensive support allows users to work with virtually any network communication.

Scripting Capabilities: Being a Python library, Scapy can be easily integrated with other Python scripts and tools. This enables automation of tasks, such as periodic traffic analysis or vulnerability scanning.

Installing Scapy

To get started with Scapy, it is necessary to install the library in your Python environment. This can be done using pip as mentioned earlier. Once installed, you can import Scapy in your Python scripts using:

python
Copy code
```
from scapy.all import *
```

Basic Usage of Scapy

Scapy's syntax is designed to be intuitive, allowing users to get started quickly. Here are some basic commands to illustrate its capabilities:

Creating a Packet: To create a simple ICMP echo request (ping) packet, you can use the following code:
python
Copy code
```
packet = IP(dst="8.8.8.8")/ICMP()
```

Sending a Packet: Once the packet is created, it can be sent to the destination using the `send` function:
python
Copy code
```
send(packet)
```

Sniffing Packets: To capture packets on the network, you can use the `sniff` function:

python
Copy code
```
sniff(prn=lambda    x:    x.summary(),
count=10)
```

This command captures ten packets and prints a summary of each one.

Analyzing Captured Packets: Scapy allows users to dissect and analyze captured packets easily. For example, to view the details of a captured packet:
python
Copy code
```
packet.show()
```

Practical Applications of Scapy

Scapy can be employed in various network security scenarios, including:

Network Scanning: Security professionals can use Scapy to perform network reconnaissance by sending crafted packets to discover hosts, services, and vulnerabilities.
Penetration Testing: Scapy enables penetration testers to simulate attacks by crafting packets that exploit known vulnerabilities in network protocols.

Traffic Analysis: Scapy's sniffing capabilities allow analysts to monitor network traffic for suspicious activity, such as unauthorized access attempts or data exfiltration.

Vulnerability Testing: By sending crafted packets, users can test the resilience of network devices and applications against specific types of attacks.

Example Use Case: ICMP Ping Sweep

One practical application of Scapy is conducting an ICMP ping sweep to identify active hosts on a network. The following code illustrates how to perform this task:

```python
Copy code
from scapy.all import *

def ping_sweep(network):
for i in range(1, 255):
ip = f"{network}.{i}"
packet = IP(dst=ip)/ICMP()
response = sr1(packet, timeout=1,
verbose=0)
if response:
print(f"Host {ip} is active")
```

```
# Perform a ping sweep on the
192.168.1.0/24 network
ping_sweep("192.168.1")
```

In this example, the script sends ICMP echo requests to all addresses in the specified subnet and prints the IP addresses of hosts that respond.

Python and Scapy provide powerful tools for network security professionals to analyze and manipulate network traffic effectively. With Python's simplicity and Scapy's robust packet handling capabilities, users can automate tasks, conduct security assessments, and develop custom solutions to enhance network security. Understanding these tools and their applications lays the foundation for more advanced techniques in network security analysis and vulnerability detection. This knowledge will be crucial as we explore specific applications of Scapy in the following chapters.

Chapter 6: Network Scanning Techniques

Introduction to Network Scanning

Network scanning is a crucial step in the network security assessment process. It involves systematically discovering active devices on a network, identifying open ports, and gathering information about the services running on those ports. This chapter explores various network scanning techniques, their purposes, methodologies, and how Python and Scapy can be used to implement these techniques effectively.

The Purpose of Network Scanning

Network scanning serves several essential functions in cybersecurity, including:

Discovery of Active Hosts: Identifying which devices are operational within a network. This information is vital for creating an inventory of assets and understanding the network landscape.

Port Scanning: Determining which ports on a host are open, closed, or filtered. Open ports can indicate active services that might be vulnerable to exploitation.

Service Identification: Gathering information about the services running on open ports, including version numbers. This helps in identifying potential vulnerabilities that could be exploited by attackers.

Vulnerability Assessment: Scanning tools can help identify known vulnerabilities associated with specific services or software versions, allowing organizations to prioritize remediation efforts.

Network Mapping: Creating a visual representation of the network architecture, which aids in understanding how devices are interconnected and where potential security risks may lie.

Types of Network Scanning Techniques

Various scanning techniques can be employed, each with unique characteristics and purposes. Here are some of the most commonly used techniques:

Ping Scanning

Ping scanning is a basic technique used to determine if a host is alive and responsive. It sends ICMP echo request packets to the target IP address and listens for echo reply packets. If a reply is received, the host is considered active.

Implementation: Using Scapy, a simple ping scan can be performed with the following code:

python

Copy code

```python
from scapy.all import ICMP, IP, sr1

def ping_scan(target):
packet = IP(dst=target)/ICMP()
response = sr1(packet, timeout=1,
verbose=0)
if response:
print(f"{target} is active")
else:
print(f"{target} is inactive")

# Example usage
ping_scan("192.168.1.1")
```

TCP Connect Scan

A TCP connect scan involves establishing a full TCP connection with the target host to determine if a port is open. This method is more intrusive and may be logged by the target's firewall or intrusion detection systems (IDS).

Process: The scanner attempts to complete the TCP three-way handshake (SYN, SYN-ACK, ACK). If the handshake is successful, the port is open; if a RST (reset) packet is received, the port is closed.

Implementation: The following code demonstrates a basic TCP connect scan using Scapy:

python

Copy code

```python
from scapy.all import IP, TCP, sr1

def tcp_connect_scan(target, port):
    packet                                    =
IP(dst=target)/TCP(dport=port,
flags='S')
    response    =    sr1(packet,    timeout=1,
verbose=0)
    if              response              and
response.haslayer(TCP):
        if response[TCP].flags  ==  0x12:   #
SYN-ACK
            print(f"Port {port} is open")
        elif response[TCP].flags == 0x14:  #
RST
            print(f"Port {port} is closed")
        else:
```

```
print(f"No response from {target}")

# Example usage
tcp_connect_scan("192.168.1.1", 80)
```

SYN Scan (Stealth Scan)

A SYN scan is a stealthier alternative to the TCP connect scan. It sends a SYN packet to the target port and waits for a response. This method does not establish a full connection, making it less likely to be logged by security systems.

Process: If a SYN-ACK is received, the port is open. If a RST packet is received, the port is closed. No response may indicate that the port is filtered.

Implementation: Here's how to perform a SYN scan with Scapy:
python
Copy code
```
from scapy.all import IP, TCP, sr1

def syn_scan(target, port):
```

```python
    packet                              =
IP(dst=target)/TCP(dport=port,
flags='S')
    response    =    sr1(packet,    timeout=1,
verbose=0)
    if              response              and
response.haslayer(TCP):
        if  response[TCP].flags  ==  0x12:    #
SYN-ACK
            print(f"Port {port} is open")
            # Optionally  send  RST  to  close  the
connection
            sr1(IP(dst=target)/TCP(dport=port,
flags='R'), timeout=1, verbose=0)
        elif  response[TCP].flags  ==  0x14:    #
RST
            print(f"Port {port} is closed")
    else:
        print(f"No response from {target}")

# Example usage
syn_scan("192.168.1.1", 80)
```

UDP Scanning

UDP scanning is more complex than TCP scanning due to the nature of the UDP protocol. Unlike TCP, UDP does not establish a connection, making it harder to determine whether a port is open or closed.

Process: To scan a UDP port, a UDP packet is sent to the target port. If the port is open, there may be no response. If it is closed, an ICMP port unreachable message is typically returned.

Implementation: A basic UDP scan can be performed as follows:
python
Copy code

```
from scapy.all import IP, UDP, sr1

def udp_scan(target, port):
packet                        =
IP(dst=target)/UDP(dport=port)
response   =   sr1(packet,   timeout=1,
verbose=0)
if response is None:
print(f"Port   {port}   is   open   or
filtered")
elif response.haslayer(ICMP):
```

```
if  response[ICMP].type  ==  3  and
response[ICMP].code == 3:
print(f"Port {port} is closed")

# Example usage
udp_scan("192.168.1.1", 53)
```

Tools for Network Scanning

In addition to using Scapy for custom scripts, there are several popular tools designed specifically for network scanning:

Nmap: Nmap is a widely used open-source tool for network discovery and security auditing. It supports various scanning techniques and provides extensive features for host discovery, port scanning, and service identification.

Masscan: Known for its speed, Masscan is capable of scanning the entire Internet in a matter of minutes. It operates similarly to Nmap but is optimized for high-speed scanning.

Netcat: Often referred to as the "Swiss army knife" of networking, Netcat can perform port scanning, establish connections, and transfer files. It's a versatile tool for network diagnostics and exploration.

Ethical Considerations

Network scanning must be conducted ethically and legally. Unauthorized scanning can be perceived as a malicious activity, leading to legal repercussions or conflicts with network administrators. Best practices include:

Permission: Always obtain explicit permission from the network owner or administrator before conducting scans.
Documentation: Keep detailed records of the scanning process, including the objectives, methods used, and results.
Impact Awareness: Be aware of the potential impact of scanning on network performance and stability. Use scanning tools and techniques that minimize disruption to ongoing operations.

Practical Applications of Network Scanning

Network scanning is used in various scenarios, including:

Security Assessments: Organizations conduct regular scans to identify vulnerabilities in their networks and services, allowing them to prioritize remediation efforts.
Inventory Management: Network scans help create an accurate inventory of devices and services, aiding in asset management and compliance efforts.

Incident Response: During a security incident, scanning can assist in identifying compromised hosts or services and help in isolating affected systems.

Network scanning is a foundational technique in network security assessments, enabling the discovery of active hosts, open ports, and running services. By understanding various scanning techniques and their applications, security professionals can effectively identify vulnerabilities and enhance their organization's security posture. Utilizing tools like Python and Scapy for custom scanning solutions empowers professionals to tailor their assessments to specific needs, ensuring a comprehensive understanding of their network environments. As we delve deeper into network security practices, this knowledge will be instrumental in effectively identifying and mitigating potential threats.

Chapter 7: Vulnerability Assessment Techniques

Introduction to Vulnerability Assessment

Vulnerability assessment is a systematic process of identifying, classifying, and prioritizing vulnerabilities in a system, application, or network. This critical component of cybersecurity helps organizations understand their security posture, assess the risks posed by identified vulnerabilities, and implement appropriate remediation measures. In this chapter, we will explore various vulnerability assessment techniques, methodologies, and how tools like Python and Scapy can be used to facilitate these processes.

The Importance of Vulnerability Assessment

Conducting regular vulnerability assessments is vital for several reasons:

Risk Identification: Organizations can proactively identify potential weaknesses in their systems and applications, allowing them to address issues before they can be exploited by attackers.

Compliance Requirements: Many regulatory frameworks, such as PCI DSS, HIPAA, and GDPR, require organizations to perform regular vulnerability assessments to ensure compliance and protect sensitive data.

Threat Intelligence: Vulnerability assessments provide valuable data that can inform threat intelligence efforts, enabling organizations to stay ahead of emerging threats.

Security Improvement: By identifying vulnerabilities, organizations can prioritize security improvements and allocate resources effectively to strengthen their defenses.

Types of Vulnerability Assessment Techniques

Several techniques can be employed during vulnerability assessments, each with its unique focus and methodologies. Here are some of the most commonly used techniques:

Automated Scanning

Automated scanning is one of the most widely used techniques for vulnerability assessment. It involves using specialized tools to scan systems and networks for known vulnerabilities.

Tools: There are numerous automated vulnerability scanning tools available, including Nessus, OpenVAS, and Qualys. These tools utilize databases of known vulnerabilities and employ various techniques to identify potential weaknesses in systems.

Implementation: While specific implementations may vary by tool, the general process involves:

Configuring the scanner with target IP addresses and scanning parameters.

Running the scan and analyzing the results.

Generating reports detailing identified vulnerabilities, risk levels, and recommended remediation steps.

Limitations: Automated scans can sometimes produce false positives or miss certain vulnerabilities, especially if they rely on signature-based detection methods. Therefore, it's crucial to complement automated scanning with manual techniques.

Manual Assessment

Manual vulnerability assessments involve human analysis and verification of vulnerabilities identified through automated tools or through other means. This approach allows for a more in-depth understanding of the environment and potential risks.

Process: A manual assessment typically involves:
Reviewing the results of automated scans and identifying critical vulnerabilities.

Conducting additional testing, such as penetration testing or code reviews, to verify the existence of vulnerabilities.

Evaluating the impact and likelihood of exploitation for each vulnerability.

Advantages: Manual assessments can uncover vulnerabilities that automated tools might miss, such as logical flaws in applications or misconfigurations that do not have known signatures.

Challenges: Manual assessments can be time-consuming and require skilled personnel with expertise in identifying and analyzing vulnerabilities.

Penetration Testing

Penetration testing, often referred to as "pen testing," is a more aggressive form of vulnerability assessment that involves simulating real-world attacks to evaluate the security of a system or network.

Approach: Penetration testing can be categorized into several approaches:

Black Box Testing: Testers have no prior knowledge of the system and must discover vulnerabilities using their skills and tools.

White Box Testing: Testers have full knowledge of the system, including access to source code and documentation, allowing for a comprehensive assessment.

Gray Box Testing: Testers have partial knowledge of the system, providing a middle ground between black and white box testing.

Execution: A typical penetration test involves:

Planning and scoping the engagement to determine the rules of engagement and goals.

Reconnaissance to gather information about the target.

Scanning for vulnerabilities and exploiting identified weaknesses.

Reporting findings and providing remediation recommendations.

Benefits: Penetration testing provides a realistic view of the organization's security posture and helps identify critical vulnerabilities that could be exploited by attackers.

Configuration Review

Configuration reviews involve examining the configurations of systems, applications, and devices to identify security weaknesses that may arise from improper settings or defaults.

Key Areas of Focus: Common areas to review include:

Network device configurations (e.g., routers, firewalls)

Operating system settings

Application security configurations (e.g., web servers, databases)

Tools: Tools like Lynis and CIS-CAT can assist in performing automated configuration assessments based on best practices and security benchmarks.

Process: A configuration review typically involves:

Establishing a baseline configuration against which to compare.

Analyzing system configurations for deviations from best practices.

Identifying potential risks and providing remediation recommendations.

Code Review

Code reviews are a vital technique for assessing the security of applications by analyzing the source code for vulnerabilities and weaknesses.

Approaches: Code reviews can be manual or automated:

Manual Code Review: Security professionals examine the code line by line to identify vulnerabilities, such as injection flaws, insecure data handling, and poor authentication mechanisms.

Static Application Security Testing (SAST): Automated tools scan the source code to identify potential security issues without executing the code.

Benefits: Conducting code reviews early in the development process helps identify vulnerabilities before they make it into production, reducing the overall cost and effort required to fix issues later.

Using Python and Scapy for Vulnerability Assessment

Python and Scapy can be effectively utilized to automate and enhance vulnerability assessment processes. Here are some ways to leverage these tools:

Scripted Scanning

Python scripts can be developed to automate various aspects of vulnerability scanning. For example, you can create a script that combines network scanning techniques with vulnerability identification:

python
Copy code

```
from scapy.all import *
import nmap

def scan_network(target):
# Perform a ping sweep to find active hosts
ans, _ = sr(IP(dst=target)/ICMP(),
timeout=2, verbose=0)
active_hosts = [rcv.psrc for snd, rcv
in ans]
```

```python
# Create a port scanner instance
nm = nmap.PortScanner()

# Scan each active host for open ports
for host in active_hosts:
    print(f"Scanning {host}...")
    nm.scan(host, arguments='-sS -p 1-1000')  # SYN scan on first 1000 ports
    print(nm[host]['tcp'])

# Example usage
scan_network("192.168.1.0/24")
```

This script first discovers active hosts on the network and then uses Nmap (a powerful network scanning tool) to scan for open ports on those hosts.

Integrating Vulnerability Databases

Python can be used to access vulnerability databases, such as the National Vulnerability Database (NVD) or Common Vulnerabilities and Exposures (CVE) database. This integration allows security professionals to cross-reference detected services and versions with known vulnerabilities.

python
Copy code

```python
import requests

def check_vulnerability(cve_id):
    url = f"https://services.nvd.nist.gov/rest/json/cve/{cve_id}"
    response = requests.get(url)
    return response.json()

# Example usage
vulnerability_data = check_vulnerability("CVE-2021-34527")
print(vulnerability_data)
```

This code snippet demonstrates how to retrieve CVE data using the NVD API, which can be useful for assessing whether any vulnerabilities exist for identified services.

Prioritizing Vulnerabilities

Once vulnerabilities have been identified, it is essential to prioritize them based on risk factors. Common frameworks for prioritization include:

CVSS (Common Vulnerability Scoring System): CVSS provides a standardized method for rating the severity of vulnerabilities. Scores range from 0 to 10, with higher scores indicating greater severity.

Business Impact Analysis: Organizations should consider the potential impact of a vulnerability on their specific environment. This includes factors such as data sensitivity, regulatory compliance, and the criticality of affected systems.

Reporting and Remediation

A critical aspect of vulnerability assessment is effectively communicating findings to stakeholders. A well-structured report should include:

Executive Summary: An overview of the assessment, including the scope, objectives, and high-level findings.

Detailed Findings: A comprehensive list of identified vulnerabilities, categorized by severity, along with descriptions and evidence.

Remediation Recommendations: Practical steps for mitigating identified vulnerabilities, including patches, configuration changes, or process improvements.

Follow-Up Actions: Suggestions for future assessments, monitoring, and ongoing security practices to enhance the organization's security posture.

Vulnerability assessment is a vital process for identifying and mitigating risks within an organization's systems and networks. By employing various techniques, including automated scanning, manual assessments, penetration testing, configuration reviews, and code reviews, security professionals can gain a comprehensive understanding of their security posture. Utilizing tools like Python and Scapy enhances the effectiveness of vulnerability assessments, enabling automation and integration with external resources. Prioritizing vulnerabilities based on risk factors and communicating findings effectively are essential for implementing successful remediation strategies and maintaining a robust security posture. As we continue to explore advanced security practices, understanding vulnerability assessment techniques will be integral to safeguarding critical assets against evolving threats.

Chapter 8: Exploitation Techniques

Introduction to Exploitation

Exploitation refers to the process of taking advantage of vulnerabilities in systems, applications, or networks to gain unauthorized access or perform malicious activities. This chapter delves into various exploitation techniques commonly used in cybersecurity, including how these techniques are implemented and how they can be tested ethically using Python and Scapy.

The Importance of Understanding Exploitation

Understanding exploitation is crucial for several reasons:

Proactive Defense: By comprehending how vulnerabilities can be exploited, security professionals can better defend against attacks by implementing appropriate security measures and patches.

Incident Response: Knowing exploitation techniques can help incident response teams identify the methods used by attackers, allowing for a more effective response and recovery process.

Security Testing: Ethical hacking and penetration testing involve simulating exploitation techniques to assess the security of systems and identify weaknesses before malicious actors can exploit them.

Types of Exploitation Techniques

Exploitation techniques can be broadly categorized into several types, each targeting different aspects of systems and networks. Here are some of the most common techniques:

Buffer Overflow Exploitation

A buffer overflow occurs when data exceeds the allocated buffer's capacity in memory, leading to the overwriting of adjacent memory locations. Attackers can exploit this vulnerability to execute arbitrary code.

How It Works: By crafting input that exceeds the buffer's limits, an attacker can manipulate the control flow of a program. This typically involves overwriting the return address of a function call with a value pointing to malicious code.

Example: Consider a vulnerable C program that does not properly check the length of user input. An attacker could send a specially crafted input that overwrites the return address and redirects execution to shellcode.

SQL Injection

SQL injection is a common web application vulnerability that allows attackers to manipulate SQL queries executed by a database.

How It Works: By injecting malicious SQL code into input fields, attackers can gain unauthorized access to databases, retrieve sensitive information, modify records, or even execute administrative operations.

Example: An attacker might input the following string into a login form:
sql
Copy code

```
' OR '1'='1'; --
```

This input could alter the SQL query to bypass authentication.

Cross-Site Scripting (XSS)

XSS is a vulnerability that allows attackers to inject malicious scripts into web pages viewed by other users.

How It Works: By injecting JavaScript or HTML code into a web application, an attacker can manipulate user sessions, steal cookies, or perform actions on behalf of the victim.

Example: An attacker could exploit a comment section of a blog to inject the following script:
html
Copy code

```
<script>alert('Hacked!');</script>
```

Remote Code Execution (RCE)

Remote code execution vulnerabilities allow attackers to execute arbitrary commands on a remote system, often leading to full system compromise.

How It Works: Attackers exploit weaknesses in software, such as unvalidated input or configuration errors, to execute commands on a target system.

Example: An attacker might find an RCE vulnerability in a web application that allows file uploads. By uploading a malicious PHP script, they can execute arbitrary code on the server.

Implementing Exploitation Techniques Using Python and Scapy

Python, combined with Scapy, can be an effective tool for simulating exploitation techniques in a controlled and ethical manner. Below, we explore how to implement some exploitation techniques using Python.

Simulating a Buffer Overflow

While actual buffer overflow exploitation is often platform-specific and requires in-depth knowledge of assembly language, Python can be used to demonstrate the concept by crafting input that would theoretically cause an overflow.

python
Copy code

```python
import subprocess

# Example buffer overflow payload
payload = b"A" * 100   # Adjust length based on buffer size

# Call a vulnerable program with the payload
subprocess.call(["vulnerable_program", payload])
```

In this example, `vulnerable_program` would be a hypothetical application that is susceptible to buffer overflow. This script simulates the process of sending excessive input to the application.

Performing SQL Injection Testing

Python's ability to interface with databases makes it a suitable choice for testing SQL injection vulnerabilities.

python
Copy code

```python
import sqlite3

def test_sql_injection(db_path):
connection = sqlite3.connect(db_path)
cursor = connection.cursor()

# Example of SQL injection payload
user_input = "' OR '1'='1'; --"
query = f"SELECT * FROM users WHERE username='{user_input}'"

cursor.execute(query)
results = cursor.fetchall()

for row in results:
print(row)

# Example usage
test_sql_injection("example.db")
```

This code attempts to demonstrate how an SQL injection might bypass authentication in a database. It's important to conduct such tests only in controlled environments with permission.

Exploiting XSS

To demonstrate XSS, one can create a simple Flask web application that is vulnerable to script injection:

python
Copy code
```
from flask import Flask, request,
render_template_string

app = Flask(__name__)

@app.route('/comment',
methods=['POST'])
def comment():
user_comment = request.form['comment']
# Vulnerable to XSS
return
render_template_string(f'<h1>Comments<
/h1><p>{user_comment}</p>')

if __name__ == '__main__':
```

```
app.run(debug=True)
```

An attacker could submit a comment containing malicious JavaScript, demonstrating how the application is vulnerable to XSS.

Ethical Considerations in Exploitation

When simulating exploitation techniques, it's essential to adhere to ethical guidelines and legal frameworks:

Obtain Permission: Always seek explicit permission from the system owner before conducting any testing that could exploit vulnerabilities.
Conduct Testing in Controlled Environments: Use isolated environments or dedicated testing servers to prevent unintended harm to production systems.
Document Findings: Keep thorough records of testing procedures, findings, and remediation recommendations to share with stakeholders.

Mitigating Exploitation Risks

Understanding exploitation techniques also empowers organizations to implement effective countermeasures. Here are some common strategies:

Input Validation: Ensure that all input is validated and sanitized to prevent buffer overflows, SQL injections, and XSS.

Use Prepared Statements: For databases, utilize prepared statements or parameterized queries to mitigate SQL injection risks.

Web Application Firewalls (WAF): Implement WAFs to filter out malicious requests and prevent common web-based attacks, including XSS and SQL injection.

Regular Software Updates: Keep software and systems updated to patch known vulnerabilities and reduce the attack surface.

Exploitation techniques are a critical aspect of understanding and defending against cybersecurity threats. By studying and simulating these techniques ethically, security professionals can enhance their defensive strategies and better protect systems and networks. Leveraging Python and Scapy for practical demonstrations of exploitation techniques provides valuable insights into potential vulnerabilities and the necessary countermeasures to mitigate risks. As we continue to explore the landscape of cybersecurity, understanding exploitation will remain essential for developing robust security practices and responding effectively to emerging threats.

Chapter 9: Penetration Testing Methodologies

Introduction to Penetration Testing

Penetration testing, often referred to as "pen testing," is a simulated cyber attack against a computer system, network, or web application to identify vulnerabilities that an attacker could exploit. This chapter provides a comprehensive overview of penetration testing methodologies, the stages involved, and how tools like Python and Scapy can be used to facilitate the process.

The Importance of Penetration Testing

Penetration testing plays a crucial role in an organization's cybersecurity strategy for several reasons:

Identifying Vulnerabilities: It helps organizations uncover weaknesses in their systems before they can be exploited by malicious actors.

Validating Security Measures: Pen testing assesses the effectiveness of existing security controls and measures, allowing organizations to verify that they function as intended.

Regulatory Compliance: Many regulatory frameworks require organizations to conduct regular penetration testing as part of their security assessments to ensure compliance with industry standards.

Improving Security Posture: By identifying and remediating vulnerabilities, organizations can enhance their overall security posture and resilience against attacks.

Phases of Penetration Testing

Penetration testing typically involves several distinct phases, each with specific objectives and activities. These phases include:

Planning and Scoping

The first phase involves defining the scope and objectives of the penetration test. This includes identifying which systems or applications will be tested, the goals of the test, and any limitations or rules of engagement.

Objectives: Determine the purpose of the test, whether it's to identify vulnerabilities, assess specific applications, or simulate a real-world attack.

Scope: Define the boundaries of the test. This may include specific IP ranges, applications, or services, and exclude certain areas to avoid disruption.

Rules of Engagement: Establish guidelines for the testing process, including communication protocols, acceptable testing methods, and reporting expectations.

Reconnaissance

Reconnaissance, or information gathering, is the phase where the penetration tester collects information about the target environment. This phase can be divided into two types: passive and active reconnaissance.

Passive Reconnaissance: Involves gathering information without directly interacting with the target. This may include searching public records, social media, and other online resources to gather details about the organization, employees, and technologies in use.

Active Reconnaissance: Involves directly interacting with the target to gather information. This may include network scanning, service discovery, and fingerprinting technologies.

Tools: Tools like Nmap, Recon-ng, and Maltego can assist in reconnaissance efforts. Python scripts can also be used to automate information gathering.

python
Copy code
```
import subprocess

def nmap_scan(target):
```

```python
command = f"nmap -sS {target}"
subprocess.run(command, shell=True)

# Example usage
nmap_scan("192.168.1.1")
```

Scanning

The scanning phase focuses on identifying live hosts, open ports, and services running on those hosts. This phase is critical for discovering vulnerabilities that can be exploited.

Network Scanning: Identifying active devices within the network using techniques like ping sweeps or ARP requests.

Port Scanning: Determining which ports are open on the target devices to understand potential entry points for exploitation.

Service Fingerprinting: Identifying the specific services and versions running on open ports to assess their vulnerabilities.

Tools: In addition to Nmap, tools like Nessus and OpenVAS can be used for vulnerability scanning.

Exploitation

The exploitation phase involves actively attempting to exploit identified vulnerabilities to gain unauthorized access to systems or data. This phase aims to demonstrate the potential impact of vulnerabilities.

Exploitation Techniques: Techniques may include SQL injection, buffer overflows, and cross-site scripting, among others.

Tools and Scripting: Python can be used to script exploits or automate the process of exploiting vulnerabilities. For example, a simple SQL injection script could be written to test a vulnerable web application.

python
Copy code
```python
import requests

def sql_injection_attack(url):
payload = "' OR '1'='1'; --"
response                             =
requests.get(f"{url}?username={payload}")
print(response.text)

# Example usage
```

```
sql_injection_attack("http://example.c
om/login")
```

Post-Exploitation

Once access has been gained, the post-exploitation phase focuses on determining the value of the compromised system and maintaining access. This phase often includes:

Privilege Escalation: Attempting to gain higher levels of access within the compromised system or network.
Data Exfiltration: Assessing the potential for data theft or unauthorized access to sensitive information.
Maintaining Access: Setting up backdoors or other means of re-entry into the system for future access.
Documentation: Keeping detailed notes on actions taken during this phase to inform the final reporting.

Reporting

The final phase of penetration testing involves compiling findings into a comprehensive report. This report should be clear, actionable, and tailored to the audience, whether they are technical staff, management, or executives.

Executive Summary: A high-level overview of the assessment, including key findings and recommendations.

Detailed Findings: A comprehensive list of identified vulnerabilities, exploitation attempts, and potential impacts.

Remediation Recommendations: Practical steps for mitigating identified vulnerabilities, including patches, configuration changes, and process improvements.

Follow-Up Actions: Suggestions for future assessments, ongoing monitoring, and continuous improvement efforts.

Using Python and Scapy in Penetration Testing

Python and Scapy can enhance penetration testing efforts through automation and scripting capabilities. Below are examples of how these tools can be integrated into different phases of the penetration testing process.

Automating Reconnaissance

Python can automate various reconnaissance tasks, such as DNS enumeration or gathering information from WHOIS databases.

python
Copy code
```
import subprocess
```

```python
def dns_enum(domain):
command = f"dig {domain} ANY"
result    =    subprocess.run(command,
shell=True,         capture_output=True,
text=True)
print(result.stdout)

# Example usage
dns_enum("example.com")
```

This script uses the `dig` command to perform DNS enumeration for a given domain, providing insights into available records.

Scanning with Scapy

Scapy can be employed for custom scanning tasks, allowing penetration testers to create tailored network scans.

python
Copy code
```python
from scapy.all import IP, ICMP, sr1

def ping_sweep(target_range):
```

```
for ip in target_range:
packet = IP(dst=ip)/ICMP()
response = sr1(packet, timeout=1,
verbose=0)
if response:
print(f"{ip} is active")

# Example usage
ping_sweep(["192.168.1.1",
"192.168.1.2", "192.168.1.3"])
```

This script performs a simple ping sweep across a specified range, helping identify active hosts.

Ethical Considerations in Penetration Testing

Conducting penetration tests requires adherence to ethical guidelines to ensure responsible and legal practices:

Obtain Written Permission: Always obtain explicit written consent from the system owner before conducting any testing.
Define Scope and Limitations: Clearly define the scope and limitations of the test to avoid unintended consequences or damage.

Protect Sensitive Data: Take precautions to protect sensitive data encountered during the test and ensure that it is not disclosed or misused.

Follow a Responsible Disclosure Process: If vulnerabilities are discovered, follow a responsible disclosure process to inform the organization and allow them to remediate the issues before publicizing any findings.

Penetration testing is an essential component of a robust cybersecurity strategy, providing valuable insights into vulnerabilities and risks within systems and networks. By following a structured methodology that includes planning, reconnaissance, scanning, exploitation, post-exploitation, and reporting, security professionals can effectively identify and mitigate weaknesses. Utilizing tools like Python and Scapy enhances the penetration testing process, allowing for automation and tailored approaches. Understanding and adhering to ethical considerations in penetration testing is crucial for maintaining trust and legality in cybersecurity practices. As we continue to explore advanced security techniques, mastering penetration testing methodologies will be instrumental in safeguarding critical assets against emerging threats.

Chapter 11: Using Scapy for Network Analysis

Introduction to Network Analysis

Network analysis is a fundamental aspect of cybersecurity, allowing professionals to monitor, diagnose, and secure network infrastructure. Scapy, a powerful Python library, provides tools for packet manipulation and network analysis. This chapter explores how Scapy can be utilized for various network analysis tasks, including traffic monitoring, protocol analysis, and security assessments.

The Importance of Network Analysis

Effective network analysis is critical for several reasons:

Traffic Monitoring: Continuous monitoring of network traffic helps identify unusual patterns or behaviors that may indicate security incidents.

Protocol Understanding: Understanding how different protocols operate allows security professionals to detect anomalies and potential attacks more effectively.

Incident Response: Quick analysis of network traffic during an incident can provide crucial insights into the nature of the attack and inform response strategies.

Performance Optimization: Analyzing network performance can help identify bottlenecks or misconfigurations that impact service delivery.

Key Concepts in Network Analysis

Before diving into Scapy, it's important to understand some key concepts in network analysis:

Packet Sniffing

Packet sniffing is the process of capturing and analyzing packets transmitted over a network. This technique helps in understanding the types of traffic present and identifying potential security threats.

Protocol Analysis

Protocol analysis involves examining the details of communication protocols (such as TCP, UDP, and ICMP) to ensure they are functioning correctly and securely. This analysis can uncover vulnerabilities and misconfigurations.

Traffic Flow Analysis

Traffic flow analysis focuses on the patterns and volumes of traffic on a network, helping identify anomalies or unusual behaviors that may indicate security incidents.

Scapy Overview

Scapy is a versatile Python library that enables users to create, send, and manipulate network packets. It supports a wide variety of protocols and provides a simple interface for packet crafting and analysis.

Key Features of Scapy

Packet Crafting: Scapy allows users to construct packets for a wide range of protocols, enabling custom tests and analyses.
Packet Sniffing: Scapy can capture packets in real-time, providing insights into network traffic as it occurs.
Protocol Dissection: Scapy can dissect packets to extract and analyze protocol fields, enabling detailed analysis of network communications.
Custom Scripts: Users can create custom scripts to automate tasks, making it easier to perform repetitive analyses or tests.

Setting Up Scapy

To use Scapy for network analysis, you need to install the library. This can typically be done using pip:

bash
Copy code
```
pip install scapy
```

Once installed, Scapy can be imported in Python scripts as follows:

python
Copy code
```
from scapy.all import *
```

Using Scapy for Packet Sniffing

Packet sniffing is one of the primary uses of Scapy. The following example demonstrates how to capture and analyze packets on a network:

python
Copy code
```
from scapy.all import sniff

def packet_callback(packet):
print(packet.summary())
```

```
# Capture packets and apply the
callback function
sniff(prn=packet_callback, count=10)
```

In this example, Scapy captures packets and applies the `packet_callback` function to each captured packet, printing a summary of its contents.

Filtering Captured Packets

Scapy allows you to filter captured packets based on various criteria, such as protocol type, source/destination IP, or port numbers. For instance, to capture only TCP packets, you can modify the `sniff` function:

python
Copy code
```
sniff(filter="tcp",
prn=packet_callback, count=10)
```

Analyzing Captured Packets

Once packets are captured, Scapy provides tools to analyze their contents. For example, you can dissect a captured packet to extract protocol fields:

python
Copy code
```python
def packet_analysis(packet):
if packet.haslayer(IP):
ip_layer = packet.getlayer(IP)
print(f"Source    IP:    {ip_layer.src},
Destination IP: {ip_layer.dst}")

# Capture packets and analyze them
sniff(prn=packet_analysis, count=10)
```

This script checks if the captured packet contains an IP layer and prints the source and destination IP addresses.

Protocol Analysis with Scapy

Scapy is particularly useful for analyzing specific protocols. For example, analyzing ARP traffic can help detect ARP spoofing attacks:

python
Copy code
```python
def arp_analysis(packet):
if packet.haslayer(ARP):
arp_layer = packet.getlayer(ARP)
```

```
print(f"ARP Request: {arp_layer.psrc}
is asking for {arp_layer.pdst}")

sniff(prn=arp_analysis, filter="arp",
count=10)
```

This script captures ARP packets and identifies requests, providing insights into potential spoofing attempts.

Traffic Flow Analysis

Traffic flow analysis involves examining patterns and volumes of traffic. Scapy can help gather statistics on the types of traffic flowing through a network.

python
Copy code
```
from collections import Counter

traffic_counts = Counter()

def traffic_flow_analysis(packet):
if packet.haslayer(IP):
ip_layer = packet.getlayer(IP)
traffic_counts[ip_layer.proto] += 1
```

```
sniff(prn=traffic_flow_analysis,
count=1000)

print("Traffic        Flow        Analysis
Results:")
for        proto,        count        in
traffic_counts.items():
print(f"Protocol    {proto}:    {count}
packets")
```

This code captures packets, counts occurrences of different protocols, and summarizes the results.

Using Scapy for Security Assessments

Scapy can also be used for security assessments, such as checking for open ports or performing network scans. For example, a simple port scan can be performed as follows:

python
Copy code
```
def port_scan(target, ports):
for port in ports:
```

```
packet                                =
IP(dst=target)/TCP(dport=port,
flags="S")
response   =   sr1(packet,   timeout=1,
verbose=0)
if            response            and
response.haslayer(TCP):
if  response[TCP].flags  ==  0x12:    #
SYN-ACK
print(f"Port {port} is open")
sr(IP(dst=target)/TCP(dport=port,
flags="R"),  timeout=1,  verbose=0)    #
Send RST

# Example usage
port_scan("192.168.1.1",        range(1,
1024))
```

This script performs a TCP SYN scan on specified ports to identify open services.

Ethical Considerations in Network Analysis

When conducting network analysis, it's important to adhere to ethical guidelines:

Obtain Permission: Always ensure you have authorization to analyze the network to avoid legal repercussions.

Respect Privacy: Be mindful of sensitive data that may be captured during analysis and handle it appropriately.

Conduct Tests Responsibly: Avoid disrupting normal network operations, especially in production environments.

Document Findings: Keep thorough documentation of analyses conducted, findings, and any actions taken.

Scapy is a powerful tool for network analysis, offering a range of capabilities for packet sniffing, protocol analysis, and security assessments. By leveraging its features, security professionals can gain valuable insights into network traffic, detect anomalies, and assess vulnerabilities. Understanding how to effectively use Scapy is crucial for enhancing network security and maintaining a robust defense against emerging threats. As we continue to explore advanced network security practices, the ability to analyze and interpret network traffic will remain a fundamental skill for cybersecurity professionals.

Chapter 12: Automating Security Tasks with Python

Introduction to Automation in Cybersecurity

Automation in cybersecurity refers to the use of technology to perform repetitive tasks, manage security processes, and respond to threats with minimal human intervention. This chapter explores how Python, a versatile programming language, can be used to automate various security tasks, enhancing efficiency, consistency, and effectiveness in cybersecurity operations.

The Importance of Automation in Cybersecurity

Automation plays a vital role in modern cybersecurity for several reasons:

Efficiency: Automation significantly reduces the time and effort required to complete repetitive tasks, allowing security teams to focus on more strategic activities.
Consistency: Automated processes ensure that security tasks are performed uniformly, reducing the likelihood of human error and oversight.

Scalability: As organizations grow, automated solutions can scale to manage increased security demands without requiring proportional increases in personnel.

Rapid Response: Automation enables quicker responses to incidents and vulnerabilities, helping to mitigate risks before they escalate.

Key Areas for Automation

Several areas in cybersecurity can benefit from automation through Python scripting, including:

Incident Response: Automating incident detection, analysis, and remediation processes to respond swiftly to threats.

Vulnerability Management: Automating vulnerability scanning and reporting to ensure timely identification and remediation of security gaps.

Log Analysis: Automating the analysis of log files to identify anomalies and potential security incidents.

Threat Intelligence: Collecting and processing threat intelligence data to inform security strategies and responses.

Network Monitoring: Automating the monitoring of network traffic for suspicious activities or policy violations.

Setting Up Your Python Environment

To begin automating security tasks, ensure that Python is installed on your system. You can download Python from the official website and install it following the provided instructions.

Additionally, several libraries and tools can enhance Python's capabilities for security automation:

Requests: For making HTTP requests to APIs and web services.
Paramiko: For SSH connectivity to remote servers.
Pandas: For data manipulation and analysis.
Beautiful Soup: For web scraping and parsing HTML.
Nmap: For network discovery and security auditing.

You can install these libraries using pip:

```bash
Copy code
pip install requests paramiko pandas
beautifulsoup4 python-nmap
```

Automating Incident Response

Incident response automation involves creating scripts that can detect, analyze, and remediate security incidents quickly. Below is an example of how to automate the detection of a malicious IP address using Python.

Step 1: Detecting Malicious IP Addresses

You can use threat intelligence feeds to check incoming connections against known malicious IPs.

python
Copy code
```python
import requests

def check_ip(ip):
    response = requests.get(f"https://api.ipgeolocation.io/ipcheck?apiKey=YOUR_API_KEY&ip={ip}")
    data = response.json()
    return data['security']['malicious']

# Example usage
ip_address = "192.168.1.10"
if check_ip(ip_address):
    print(f"Alert: Malicious activity detected from {ip_address}")
```

This script checks an IP address against a threat intelligence API, alerting if it's flagged as malicious.

Step 2: Automated Remediation

If a malicious IP is detected, you might want to automate the process of blocking that IP address using a firewall configuration script.

python
Copy code

```
import subprocess

def block_ip(ip):
command = f"iptables -A INPUT -s {ip} -j DROP"
subprocess.run(command, shell=True)

# Example usage
if check_ip(ip_address):
block_ip(ip_address)
```

This script uses the `iptables` command to block traffic from a detected malicious IP address.

Automating Vulnerability Management

Vulnerability management can be streamlined by automating scans and reporting. Tools like OpenVAS or

Nessus can be integrated into Python scripts to schedule scans and collect results.

python
Copy code
```
import os

def run_vulnerability_scan(target):
os.system(f"openvas -s {target}")

# Example usage
run_vulnerability_scan("192.168.1.0/24
")
```

This script triggers a vulnerability scan on the specified target range using OpenVAS.

Automating Log Analysis

Log analysis is critical for identifying security incidents. You can automate the process of analyzing logs for specific patterns or anomalies.

python
Copy code
```
import pandas as pd
```

```python
def analyze_logs(log_file):
    logs = pd.read_csv(log_file)
    # Check for failed login attempts
    failed_logins = logs[logs['status'] ==
    'failed']
    if not failed_logins.empty:
    print(f"Failed        login        attempts
    detected: {len(failed_logins)}")

# Example usage
analyze_logs("system_logs.csv")
```

This script analyzes a CSV log file for failed login attempts, providing insights into potential unauthorized access attempts.

Automating Threat Intelligence Collection

Automating the collection of threat intelligence data can help organizations stay ahead of emerging threats. You can create scripts to scrape threat intelligence feeds and store the data for analysis.

python
Copy code
```python
import requests
```

```python
from bs4 import BeautifulSoup

def collect_threat_intelligence(url):
response = requests.get(url)
soup = BeautifulSoup(response.text,
'html.parser')
threats = soup.find_all('div',
class_='threat')
for threat in threats:
print(threat.text)

# Example usage
collect_threat_intelligence("https://e
xample.com/threats")
```

This script scrapes a hypothetical threat intelligence webpage, extracting and printing threat information.

Automating Network Monitoring

Network monitoring can also be automated using Python. Below is an example of automating the monitoring of network devices for availability.

python
Copy code

```python
import os
import time

def ping_device(ip):
response = os.system(f"ping -c 1
{ip}")
return response == 0

devices              = ["192.168.1.1",
"192.168.1.2"]

while True:
for device in devices:
if ping_device(device):
print(f"{device} is online")
else:
print(f"{device} is offline")
time.sleep(60)   # Wait for 1 minute
before checking again
```

This script continuously pings specified devices and reports their availability.

Ethical Considerations in Automation

While automation can enhance security operations, it's crucial to consider ethical implications:

Obtain Permission: Always ensure you have authorization to automate security tasks in a given environment.

Respect Privacy: Be mindful of sensitive data when automating processes, especially when handling logs or user data.

Avoid Disruption: Automated tasks should be designed to avoid impacting normal operations or causing disruptions.

Maintain Transparency: Keep stakeholders informed about automated processes and their implications on security posture.

Automating security tasks with Python significantly enhances efficiency, consistency, and effectiveness in cybersecurity operations. By leveraging Python's capabilities, security professionals can automate incident response, vulnerability management, log analysis, threat intelligence collection, and network monitoring. However, it is essential to approach automation with ethical considerations in mind, ensuring that automated processes are transparent, respectful of privacy, and do not disrupt normal operations. As the cybersecurity landscape evolves, the ability to automate security tasks will remain a crucial skill for professionals seeking to protect their organizations against emerging threats.

Chapter 13: Threat Hunting and Incident Response

Introduction to Threat Hunting

Threat hunting is a proactive cybersecurity practice that involves actively searching for signs of malicious activity within an organization's network. Unlike traditional security measures that rely on automated alerts and defenses, threat hunting focuses on human analysis to identify hidden threats and respond effectively. This chapter explores the principles of threat hunting, techniques used, and how Python can facilitate these activities in conjunction with incident response processes.

The Importance of Threat Hunting

Threat hunting is critical for several reasons:

Proactive Defense: By actively searching for threats, organizations can identify and mitigate potential attacks before they escalate.

Contextual Insights: Human analysts can provide context to security alerts, distinguishing between false positives and genuine threats.

Improved Detection: Threat hunting helps improve detection capabilities by identifying indicators of compromise (IOCs) that automated systems might miss.

Incident Preparation: Insights gained from threat hunting can inform incident response planning and improve overall security posture.

Key Concepts in Threat Hunting

Before delving into the techniques and tools, it's essential to understand some key concepts in threat hunting:

Indicators of Compromise (IOCs)

IOCs are artifacts or pieces of forensic data that suggest a security breach or malicious activity. Examples include unusual network traffic patterns, file hashes, or IP addresses associated with known threats.

Threat Intelligence

Threat intelligence refers to information about current or emerging threats that can inform security strategies. It includes data on attack techniques, malware signatures, and the behaviors of threat actors.

Hypothesis-Driven Hunting

Threat hunters often work based on hypotheses about potential threats, drawing from previous incidents or intelligence. This approach allows them to focus their efforts on specific areas of concern.

Setting Up a Threat Hunting Environment

To effectively conduct threat hunting, it's important to establish a suitable environment. This typically includes:

Data Sources: Collecting data from various sources such as firewalls, intrusion detection systems (IDS), endpoint detection and response (EDR) tools, and server logs.

Analytical Tools: Utilizing analytical tools and scripting languages like Python to process and analyze the collected data.

Collaboration: Ensuring collaboration between threat hunters, incident responders, and other cybersecurity teams for comprehensive threat analysis.

Threat Hunting Techniques

Several techniques are commonly used in threat hunting, including:

Behavioral Analysis

Behavioral analysis involves examining patterns of behavior within the network to identify anomalies. By establishing baselines for normal activity, analysts can detect deviations indicative of potential threats.

Example: Monitoring user login patterns to identify unusual access attempts, such as logins from geographic locations that are not typical for the organization.

Network Traffic Analysis

Analyzing network traffic can reveal suspicious activities, such as data exfiltration or command-and-control communications. This technique often involves deep packet inspection and protocol analysis.

Example: Using Scapy to capture and analyze packets to identify unusual outbound connections.

Endpoint Analysis

Endpoint analysis involves examining endpoint devices for signs of compromise, such as unauthorized software installations or unusual processes.

Example: Using Python to analyze process lists on endpoints for known malware signatures or behaviors.

python

Copy code

```
import psutil

def check_processes():
for process in
psutil.process_iter(['pid', 'name']):
if "malicious_process_name" in
process.info['name']:
print(f"Alert: Malicious process
found: {process.info['name']} (PID:
{process.info['pid']})")

check_processes()
```

Log Analysis

Logs provide a wealth of information that can be mined for signs of malicious activity. Threat hunters often analyze logs from various sources, including web servers, application logs, and system logs.

Example: Using Python to parse and analyze logs for failed login attempts, unusual access times, or other suspicious activities.

python

Copy code

```
import pandas as pd

def analyze_logs(log_file):
logs = pd.read_csv(log_file)
suspicious_logins                =
logs[(logs['status'] == 'failed') &
(logs['timestamp'].str.contains('2024-
10-11'))]
if not suspicious_logins.empty:
print(f"Suspicious    logins    detected:
{len(suspicious_logins)}")

analyze_logs("auth_logs.csv")
```

Integrating Threat Hunting with Incident Response

Threat hunting and incident response go hand in hand. The insights gained from hunting activities can inform and enhance incident response efforts.

Identifying and Prioritizing Threats

During threat hunting, analysts may identify potential threats that require immediate attention. These findings should be prioritized based on potential impact and likelihood, allowing incident response teams to focus their efforts effectively.

Developing Incident Response Plans

The knowledge gained from threat hunting should inform the development and refinement of incident response plans. For example, if a particular attack vector is frequently identified during hunting, the organization can prepare specific response strategies for those scenarios.

Creating a Feedback Loop

Establishing a feedback loop between threat hunters and incident responders can help continuously improve threat detection and response capabilities. Lessons learned from incident response can guide future hunting efforts, and vice versa.

Tools and Frameworks for Threat Hunting

Several tools and frameworks can facilitate threat hunting:

ELK Stack: The Elastic Stack (Elasticsearch, Logstash, Kibana) is widely used for log management and analysis, allowing threat hunters to visualize data and identify patterns.

Splunk: Splunk provides powerful data analytics capabilities, enabling organizations to search, monitor, and analyze machine-generated data.

Threat Hunting Frameworks: Frameworks like MITRE ATT&CK provide a comprehensive knowledge base of adversary tactics and techniques, helping hunters understand potential threats and develop effective hunting strategies.

Using Python for Threat Hunting

Python can be a powerful ally in threat hunting activities. Here are some examples of how Python can enhance the threat hunting process:

Automating Data Collection

Python scripts can automate the collection of data from various sources, including log files, network devices, and threat intelligence feeds. This automation can streamline the initial phases of threat hunting.

python
Copy code

```python
import requests


def fetch_threat_intelligence():
```

```
response                               =
requests.get("https://threatintelligen
ce.api/threats")
return response.json()

threat_data                            =
fetch_threat_intelligence()
print(threat_data)
```

Analyzing Network Traffic

Python can be used with libraries like Scapy to analyze
network traffic for indicators of compromise.

python
Copy code
```
from scapy.all import sniff

def analyze_packet(packet):
if packet.haslayer("IP"):
ip_layer = packet["IP"]
if  ip_layer.dst  ==  "10.0.0.1":    #
Monitor specific IP
print(f"Traffic    to    sensitive    IP
detected from {ip_layer.src}")
```

```
sniff(prn=analyze_packet, filter="ip",
store=0)
```

Automating Reporting

Python scripts can automate the generation of reports based on threat hunting findings, helping teams share insights and recommendations efficiently.

python
Copy code
```
def generate_report(threats):
with open("threat_report.txt", "w") as
f:
for threat in threats:
f.write(f"Threat        identified:
{threat}\n")

threats_identified    =    ["Suspicious
login        from        192.168.1.10",
"Unauthorized access to file shares"]
generate_report(threats_identified)
```

Ethical Considerations in Threat Hunting

126

As with all cybersecurity activities, ethical considerations must guide threat hunting efforts:

Privacy Concerns: Be mindful of user privacy when collecting and analyzing data. Ensure compliance with relevant data protection regulations.

Authorization: Always obtain appropriate authorization before conducting threat hunting activities, especially in production environments.

Responsible Disclosure: If vulnerabilities are identified during hunting activities, follow responsible disclosure protocols to inform affected parties and mitigate risks.

Threat hunting is a proactive approach to cybersecurity that involves actively searching for hidden threats within an organization's network. By leveraging techniques such as behavioral analysis, network traffic analysis, endpoint analysis, and log analysis, threat hunters can identify and mitigate potential threats before they escalate. Integrating threat hunting with incident response enhances the effectiveness of security operations, enabling organizations to respond swiftly to incidents. Python serves as a valuable tool in threat hunting, automating data collection, analysis, and reporting processes. However, ethical considerations must guide all threat hunting activities to ensure responsible practices and protect user privacy. As organizations continue to face evolving threats, mastering threat hunting will be essential for maintaining a strong security posture.

Chapter 14:

Integrating Python Tools with SIEM Solutions

Introduction to Security Information and Event Management (SIEM)

Security Information and Event Management (SIEM) is a critical component of modern cybersecurity infrastructure. SIEM solutions collect, analyze, and correlate security data from various sources within an organization, providing real-time visibility into security events and incidents. This chapter explores how Python can be integrated with SIEM solutions to enhance their capabilities, automate workflows, and improve overall security monitoring and incident response.

The Role of SIEM in Cybersecurity

SIEM systems serve several essential functions in cybersecurity:

Data Collection: SIEM solutions aggregate logs and security data from multiple sources, including firewalls, intrusion detection systems (IDS), servers, and applications.

Real-Time Monitoring: SIEM tools provide real-time visibility into security events, enabling organizations to detect and respond to incidents swiftly.

Event Correlation: SIEM systems analyze and correlate events from different sources to identify patterns that may indicate security threats.

Reporting and Compliance: SIEM solutions generate reports for compliance with regulatory requirements and provide insights into security posture.

Common SIEM Solutions

Several SIEM solutions are widely used in the industry, each with its features and capabilities. Some popular SIEM platforms include:

Splunk: A powerful platform for searching, monitoring, and analyzing machine-generated data.

IBM QRadar: A comprehensive SIEM solution that offers advanced threat detection and incident response capabilities.

ArcSight: A solution that provides real-time threat detection, incident response, and compliance reporting.

LogRhythm: A security intelligence platform that combines SIEM capabilities with advanced analytics.

Why Integrate Python with SIEM?

Integrating Python with SIEM solutions offers numerous benefits:

Automation: Python can automate repetitive tasks, such as data ingestion, report generation, and alert management, improving efficiency.

Custom Data Processing: Python allows for the creation of custom scripts to preprocess and analyze data before it enters the SIEM, enhancing detection capabilities.

Extending SIEM Functionality: Python can be used to develop custom integrations with other tools, APIs, and data sources, enriching the SIEM's capabilities.

Rapid Prototyping: Python's simplicity allows for quick development and testing of new security workflows and analysis techniques.

Setting Up Your Python Environment for SIEM Integration

Before integrating Python with a SIEM solution, ensure that you have the necessary tools and libraries installed. Commonly used libraries include:

Requests: For making HTTP requests to SIEM APIs.

Pandas: For data manipulation and analysis.

PySnmp: For SNMP communication with network devices.

SQLAlchemy: For database interactions, if needed.

Install these libraries using pip:

bash
Copy code

```
pip install requests pandas pysnmp
sqlalchemy
```

Using Python to Collect Data for SIEM

One of the primary functions of SIEM solutions is data collection. Python scripts can be used to automate the collection of logs and events from various sources.

Example: Collecting Logs from a Web Server

You can use Python to collect logs from a web server and send them to a SIEM solution via an API.

python
Copy code

```
import requests

def send_logs_to_siem(log_data):
    url = "https://siem.example.com/api/logs"
    headers = {'Authorization': 'Bearer
YOUR_API_KEY'}
```

```python
response = requests.post(url,
json=log_data, headers=headers)
return response.status_code

# Example usage
log_data = {
"timestamp": "2024-10-11T10:00:00Z",
"source": "web_server",
"message": "User accessed the
homepage."
}

status_code =
send_logs_to_siem(log_data)
if status_code == 200:
print("Logs sent to SIEM
successfully.")
```

This script collects log data and sends it to the SIEM via an API endpoint.

Automating Alert Management

Python can also be used to automate the management of alerts generated by the SIEM. This includes acknowledging, escalating, or remediating alerts based on predefined criteria.

Example: Acknowledging Alerts

You can create a script that acknowledges alerts in the SIEM based on certain conditions.

python
Copy code
```python
def acknowledge_alert(alert_id):
    url = f"https://siem.example.com/api/alerts/{alert_id}/acknowledge"
    headers = {'Authorization': 'Bearer YOUR_API_KEY'}
    response = requests.post(url, headers=headers)
    return response.status_code

# Example usage
alert_id = "12345"
status_code = acknowledge_alert(alert_id)
if status_code == 200:
```

```
print(f"Alert {alert_id} acknowledged
successfully.")
```

This script acknowledges a specific alert in the SIEM, streamlining incident management.

Custom Data Processing with Python

Custom data processing is crucial for enriching the data that enters the SIEM. Python can be used to preprocess logs, perform transformations, and enrich data with additional context.

Example: Enriching Logs with Threat Intelligence

Integrating threat intelligence into logs before sending them to the SIEM can enhance detection capabilities.

python
Copy code
```
def
enrich_log_with_threat_intel(log_data)
:
threat_intel                          =
fetch_threat_intelligence()           #
Function to fetch threat intelligence
```

135

```
if        log_data['source_ip']        in
threat_intel:
log_data['threat_level'] = "High"
else:
log_data['threat_level'] = "Low"
return log_data

# Example usage
log_data = {
"timestamp": "2024-10-11T10:00:00Z",
"source_ip": "192.168.1.10",
"message": "User accessed a sensitive
area."
}

enriched_log                          =
enrich_log_with_threat_intel(log_data)
send_logs_to_siem(enriched_log)
```

This script checks if the source IP of the log data is in the threat intelligence database and enriches the log accordingly.

Creating Custom Dashboards and Reports

Python can be used to create custom dashboards and reports that visualize data from the SIEM. Libraries such as Matplotlib and Plotly can be used for data visualization.

Example: Generating a Custom Report

You can create a simple report summarizing alerts from the SIEM using Python.

python
Copy code
```python
import pandas as pd

def generate_alert_report(alerts):
df = pd.DataFrame(alerts)
report = df.groupby('severity').count()
report.to_csv("alert_report.csv")

# Example usage
alerts = [
{"id": "1", "severity": "High"},
{"id": "2", "severity": "Medium"},
{"id": "3", "severity": "High"},
]
```

```
generate_alert_report(alerts)
print("Alert       report       generated
successfully.")
```

This script generates a report summarizing the number of alerts by severity and saves it as a CSV file.

Integrating Python with SIEM APIs

Most SIEM solutions provide APIs that allow for integration and data exchange. Python's `requests` library makes it easy to interact with these APIs.

Example: Querying the SIEM for Alerts

You can use Python to query the SIEM for recent alerts and take appropriate actions based on the results.

```python
Copy code
def fetch_recent_alerts():
    url                           =
"https://siem.example.com/api/alerts/r
ecent"
    headers = {'Authorization': 'Bearer
YOUR_API_KEY'}
```

```
response        =        requests.get(url,
headers=headers)
return response.json()

# Example usage
recent_alerts = fetch_recent_alerts()
print(f"Recent                    alerts:
{recent_alerts}")
```

This script retrieves recent alerts from the SIEM, providing insights into potential threats.

Ethical Considerations in SIEM Integration

As with any cybersecurity practice, ethical considerations must guide the integration of Python tools with SIEM solutions:

Data Privacy: Ensure compliance with data protection regulations when handling and processing security data.
Authorization: Obtain appropriate authorization before accessing or modifying SIEM data and configurations.
Transparency: Maintain transparency with stakeholders regarding automated processes and data handling practices.

Integrating Python tools with SIEM solutions enhances the capabilities of security monitoring and incident response. By automating data collection, alert management, and custom data processing, organizations can improve efficiency and responsiveness to security threats. Python's versatility allows for rapid prototyping and development of custom integrations, enriching the SIEM's functionality. However, ethical considerations must guide all integration efforts to ensure responsible practices in handling sensitive security data. As the cybersecurity landscape continues to evolve, the ability to leverage Python in SIEM integrations will remain an essential skill for security professionals.

Chapter 15: Advanced Threat Detection Techniques with Python

Introduction to Advanced Threat Detection

As cyber threats evolve in complexity and sophistication, traditional security measures often fall short in effectively identifying and mitigating these risks. Advanced threat detection techniques are essential for staying ahead of malicious actors. This chapter explores various advanced detection methods, leveraging Python to enhance threat identification and response capabilities.

The Need for Advanced Threat Detection

The increasing frequency and severity of cyberattacks necessitate advanced detection techniques due to several factors:

Evolving Threat Landscape: Attackers continually adapt their tactics, making it essential for security teams to employ innovative detection strategies.

Complex Attack Vectors: Many modern attacks, such as Advanced Persistent Threats (APTs), utilize multiple stages and techniques to evade detection.

Volume of Data: The sheer volume of logs and events generated in modern IT environments can overwhelm traditional detection methods, necessitating automated, intelligent approaches.

Insider Threats: Identifying malicious activities initiated by insiders can be particularly challenging, requiring nuanced detection techniques.

Key Concepts in Advanced Threat Detection

Before delving into specific techniques, it's crucial to understand some key concepts related to advanced threat detection:

Anomaly Detection

Anomaly detection involves identifying patterns in data that deviate significantly from expected behavior. This technique is particularly useful for spotting unusual activities that may indicate a security threat.

Machine Learning

Machine learning (ML) can enhance threat detection by allowing systems to learn from historical data and identify patterns that signify malicious behavior.

Algorithms can be trained to recognize anomalies or classify data based on features.

Threat Intelligence

Integrating threat intelligence feeds into detection systems enriches data with contextual information about known threats, improving the accuracy and speed of detection efforts.

Setting Up Python for Advanced Detection

To effectively implement advanced threat detection techniques using Python, ensure that you have the necessary libraries installed:

NumPy: For numerical computations and data manipulation.
Pandas: For data analysis and manipulation.
Scikit-learn: For machine learning algorithms.
Matplotlib/Seaborn: For data visualization.

You can install these libraries using pip:

bash
Copy code

```
pip install numpy pandas scikit-learn
matplotlib seaborn
```

Anomaly Detection Using Statistical Methods

Statistical methods are commonly used for anomaly detection. By analyzing historical data, security analysts can establish a baseline of normal behavior and identify deviations.

Example: Identifying Anomalous Login Attempts

The following example demonstrates how to identify anomalous login attempts based on user login times.

```python
Copy code
import pandas as pd

# Load login data
logins = pd.read_csv("login_data.csv")

# Convert timestamp to datetime
logins['timestamp']               =
pd.to_datetime(logins['timestamp'])

# Extract hour from timestamp
logins['hour']                    =
logins['timestamp'].dt.hour
```

```python
# Calculate mean and standard
deviation of login hours
mean_hour = logins['hour'].mean()
std_hour = logins['hour'].std()

# Identify anomalous login attempts
anomalous_logins                    =
logins[(logins['hour'] < mean_hour - 3
* std_hour) |
(logins['hour'] > mean_hour + 3 *
std_hour)]

print("Anomalous login attempts:")
print(anomalous_logins)
```

This script identifies login attempts that occur at unusual hours, which may indicate suspicious behavior.

Machine Learning for Threat Detection

Machine learning algorithms can be employed for various detection tasks, such as classifying events or predicting malicious activities. Below is an example of how to use a simple machine learning model for classification.

Example: Classifying Network Traffic

You can use a machine learning model to classify network traffic as either "normal" or "malicious" based on features such as packet size, protocol, and source IP.

python
Copy code
```
from sklearn.model_selection import
train_test_split
from sklearn.ensemble import
RandomForestClassifier
import pandas as pd

# Load network traffic data
data                             =
pd.read_csv("network_traffic.csv")

# Define features and labels
features    =    data[['packet_size',
'protocol', 'source_ip']]
labels = data['label']  # 'normal' or
'malicious'

# Split the data into training and
testing sets
```

```python
X_train, X_test, y_train, y_test =
train_test_split(features,      labels,
test_size=0.2, random_state=42)

# Train a Random Forest classifier
classifier = RandomForestClassifier()
classifier.fit(X_train, y_train)

# Evaluate the model
accuracy = classifier.score(X_test,
y_test)
print(f"Model accuracy: {accuracy *
100:.2f}%")
```

This script trains a Random Forest classifier on network traffic data and evaluates its accuracy in classifying traffic as normal or malicious.

Integrating Threat Intelligence

Incorporating threat intelligence into detection mechanisms can significantly enhance their effectiveness. Threat intelligence provides context and enriches data, allowing for more informed decision-making.

Example: Enriching Logs with Threat Intelligence

You can enhance log data with threat intelligence by cross-referencing IP addresses against a threat feed.

python
Copy code
```
import requests

def
enrich_log_with_threat_intelligence(lo
gs):
threat_feed                          =
requests.get("https://threatfeed.examp
le.com/api/ips").json()
threat_ips                           =
set(threat_feed['malicious_ips'])

for log in logs:
if log['source_ip'] in threat_ips:
log['threat_level'] = "High"
else:
log['threat_level'] = "Low"
return logs

# Example usage
```

```
logs = [
{"timestamp":   "2024-10-11T10:00:00Z",
"source_ip":           "192.168.1.10",
"message":      "Accessed      sensitive
data."},
{"timestamp":   "2024-10-11T10:05:00Z",
"source_ip": "203.0.113.5", "message":
"Unusual login attempt."}
]

enriched_logs                         =
enrich_log_with_threat_intelligence(lo
gs)
print(enriched_logs)
```

This script fetches threat intelligence data and enriches log entries with threat levels based on known malicious IP addresses.

Behavioral Analysis for Threat Detection

Behavioral analysis focuses on understanding user and entity behavior to identify anomalies indicative of potential threats.

Example: User Behavior Analysis

You can analyze user behavior to detect anomalies, such as unusual access patterns or data usage.

python
Copy code
```
import pandas as pd

# Load user activity data
activity_data = pd.read_csv("user_activity.csv")

# Calculate average data usage per user
average_usage = activity_data.groupby('user_id')['data _usage'].mean()

# Identify users with anomalously high data usage
anomalous_users = activity_data[activity_data['data_usage'] > average_usage + 3 * activity_data['data_usage'].std()]

print("Anomalous users:")
```

```
print(anomalous_users)
```

This script identifies users whose data usage significantly exceeds the average, potentially indicating malicious activities such as data exfiltration.

Threat Detection Using Honeypots

Honeypots are decoy systems designed to lure attackers and detect malicious activities. Integrating honeypots into your network can provide valuable insights into attack methodologies.

Example: Analyzing Honeypot Data

You can analyze data collected from a honeypot to identify attack patterns.

python
Copy code
```
import pandas as pd

# Load honeypot logs
honeypot_logs                               =
pd.read_csv("honeypot_logs.csv")

# Analyze attack vectors
```

```
attack_counts                              =
honeypot_logs['attack_vector'].value_c
ounts()

print("Attack vectors detected:")
print(attack_counts)
```

This script analyzes honeypot logs to identify the most common attack vectors, providing insights into potential threats.

Visualizing Threat Detection Results

Data visualization is essential for interpreting threat detection results and communicating findings to stakeholders. Libraries such as Matplotlib and Seaborn can be used to create informative visualizations.

Example: Visualizing Anomalous Activity

You can create visualizations to represent the frequency of anomalous activities over time.

python
Copy code
```
import matplotlib.pyplot as plt
import pandas as pd
```

```python
# Load anomalous activity data
anomalous_data                =
pd.read_csv("anomalous_activity.csv")

# Plot frequency of anomalies over
time
plt.figure(figsize=(10, 5))
plt.plot(anomalous_data['timestamp'],
anomalous_data['anomaly_count'],
marker='o')
plt.title('Anomalous    Activity    Over
Time')
plt.xlabel('Timestamp')
plt.ylabel('Number of Anomalies')
plt.xticks(rotation=45)
plt.tight_layout()
plt.show()
```

This script visualizes the frequency of anomalous activities over time, aiding in the analysis of trends and patterns.

Ethical Considerations in Advanced Threat Detection

When implementing advanced threat detection techniques, ethical considerations are paramount:

Privacy Concerns: Ensure compliance with data protection regulations when collecting and analyzing user data.

Transparency: Maintain transparency with stakeholders regarding detection methods and data handling practices.

Responsible Use of Threat Intelligence: Use threat intelligence responsibly, ensuring that data is accurate and used appropriately.

Advanced threat detection techniques are essential for identifying and mitigating modern cyber threats. By leveraging anomaly detection, machine learning, threat intelligence, behavioral analysis, and honeypots, security teams can enhance their detection capabilities. Python serves as a powerful tool in implementing these techniques, enabling automation, data analysis, and visualization. However, ethical considerations must guide all detection efforts to ensure responsible practices in handling sensitive information. As cyber threats continue to evolve, mastering advanced detection techniques will be critical for maintaining robust cybersecurity defenses.

Chapter 16:

Automating Incident Response with Python

Introduction to Incident Response Automation

Incident response (IR) is a crucial component of cybersecurity, focused on identifying, managing, and mitigating security incidents. Given the increasing complexity and volume of cyber threats, automating aspects of the incident response process has become essential for organizations. This chapter explores how Python can be leveraged to automate incident response activities, enhance efficiency, and improve response times.

The Importance of Incident Response Automation

Automating incident response processes offers several key benefits:

Speed: Automation reduces the time taken to detect, analyze, and respond to incidents, allowing organizations to address threats more swiftly.

Consistency: Automated processes ensure that responses are standardized, minimizing the risk of human error during critical situations.

Scalability: As organizations grow, the volume of security events increases. Automation allows security teams to scale their response capabilities without proportionally increasing their resources.

Efficiency: Automating repetitive tasks frees up security analysts to focus on more complex issues, improving overall team productivity.

Key Components of Incident Response Automation

Effective incident response automation involves several key components:

Incident Detection

Detecting security incidents in real time is the first step in the incident response process. Automated tools can monitor systems for anomalies, alerts, and predefined indicators of compromise (IOCs).

Triage and Analysis

Once an incident is detected, automated systems can prioritize and analyze it based on predefined criteria, such as severity and impact. This step is critical for determining the appropriate response.

Response and Remediation

Automated response mechanisms can execute predefined actions to contain and mitigate threats. This may include isolating affected systems, blocking malicious IP addresses, or executing remediation scripts.

Reporting and Documentation

Automated systems can generate reports and documentation for incidents, capturing essential details for compliance and post-incident analysis.

Setting Up Your Python Environment for Incident Response Automation

To automate incident response tasks using Python, ensure you have the necessary libraries installed:

Requests: For making HTTP requests to APIs.
Pandas: For data manipulation and analysis.
Subprocess: For executing system commands.
Logging: For logging activities and events.

You can install the required libraries using pip:

bash
Copy code
```
pip install requests pandas
```

Automating Incident Detection

Automating incident detection is essential for proactive incident management. Python scripts can be used to monitor logs, system metrics, and network traffic.

Example: Monitoring System Logs for Anomalies

The following example demonstrates how to monitor system logs for unusual entries that may indicate an incident.

python
Copy code
```
import pandas as pd

def monitor_logs(log_file):
logs = pd.read_csv(log_file)
suspicious_logs                        =
logs[logs['severity'] == 'high']

if not suspicious_logs.empty:
print("Suspicious logs detected:")
```

159

```
print(suspicious_logs)

# Example usage
monitor_logs("system_logs.csv")
```

This script monitors system logs and identifies any entries marked with high severity, alerting security teams to potential incidents.

Automating Triage and Analysis

Once an incident is detected, triaging and analyzing the incident is crucial for determining the appropriate response. Automation can streamline this process.

Example: Automating Incident Triage

You can automate the triage process by categorizing incidents based on their severity and potential impact.

python
Copy code
```
def triage_incidents(incident_data):
high_severity                      =
incident_data[incident_data['severity'
] == 'high']
```

```python
medium_severity                         =
incident_data[incident_data['severity'
] == 'medium']

print(f"High    severity    incidents:
{len(high_severity)}")
print(f"Medium   severity   incidents:
{len(medium_severity)}")

# Example usage
incident_data = pd.DataFrame({
'incident_id': [1, 2, 3],
'severity': ['high', 'medium', 'low']
})

triage_incidents(incident_data)
```

This script categorizes incidents based on severity, allowing the security team to prioritize their response efforts.

Automating Response and Remediation

Automated response mechanisms can help contain and remediate incidents swiftly. Python scripts can execute predefined actions based on the type of incident.

Example: Blocking a Malicious IP Address

You can automate the process of blocking a malicious IP address identified during an incident.

python
Copy code
```python
import subprocess

def block_ip(ip_address):
try:
subprocess.run(["iptables",    "-A",
"INPUT",   "-s",   ip_address,   "-j",
"DROP"], check=True)
print(f"Blocked    IP    address:
{ip_address}")
except   subprocess.CalledProcessError
as e:
print(f"Error blocking IP: {e}")

# Example usage
malicious_ip = "203.0.113.5"
block_ip(malicious_ip)
```

This script uses the `iptables` command to block a specified IP address, containing the threat.

Automating Reporting and Documentation

Documenting incidents is vital for compliance and post-incident analysis. Automation can help streamline this process.

Example: Generating Incident Reports

You can create a script to generate incident reports based on recorded incidents.

```python
Copy code
def generate_incident_report(incidents):
    report_file = "incident_report.txt"
    with open(report_file, "w") as f:
        for incident in incidents:
            f.write(f"Incident                ID: {incident['incident_id']},    Severity: {incident['severity']}\n")
```

```python
print(f"Incident report generated: {report_file}")

# Example usage
incidents = [
{"incident_id": 1, "severity": "high"},
{"incident_id": 2, "severity": "medium"},
]

generate_incident_report(incidents)
```

This script generates a simple text report documenting incidents, helping security teams keep records for future reference.

Integrating with SIEM Solutions

Many organizations use Security Information and Event Management (SIEM) solutions to monitor and manage incidents. Python can be integrated with SIEM APIs to automate incident response processes.

Example: Sending Incident Alerts to SIEM

You can automate the process of sending alerts to a SIEM system for further analysis.

python
Copy code

```python
import requests

def send_alert_to_siem(incident):
    url = "https://siem.example.com/api/alerts"
    headers = {'Authorization': 'Bearer YOUR_API_KEY'}
    response = requests.post(url, json=incident, headers=headers)
    return response.status_code

# Example usage
incident = {
"incident_id": 1,
"severity": "high",
"description": "Malicious login attempt detected."
}
```

```
status_code                    =
send_alert_to_siem(incident)
if status_code == 200:
print("Incident alert sent to SIEM
successfully.")
```

This script sends incident alerts to a SIEM solution, ensuring that critical incidents are logged and monitored.

Using Machine Learning for Incident Response

Machine learning can enhance incident response automation by predicting potential incidents and automating responses based on historical data.

Example: Predicting Incidents Using Machine Learning

You can train a machine learning model to predict potential incidents based on historical incident data.

python
Copy code
```
from sklearn.model_selection import
train_test_split
from sklearn.ensemble import
RandomForestClassifier
import pandas as pd
```

```python
# Load historical incident data
data                              =
pd.read_csv("historical_incidents.csv"
)

# Define features and labels
features        =        data[['feature1',
'feature2', 'feature3']]
labels = data['incident_occurred']    #
1 for yes, 0 for no

# Split the data into training and
testing sets
X_train, X_test, y_train, y_test =
train_test_split(features,      labels,
test_size=0.2, random_state=42)

# Train a Random Forest classifier
model = RandomForestClassifier()
model.fit(X_train, y_train)

# Evaluate the model
accuracy = model.score(X_test, y_test)
```

```
print(f"Model  accuracy:  {accuracy  *
100:.2f}%")
```

This script trains a machine learning model to predict incidents based on historical data, potentially automating future incident response.

Ethical Considerations in Incident Response Automation

While automating incident response offers many benefits, it is crucial to adhere to ethical considerations:

Privacy: Ensure that automated processes comply with data protection regulations and respect user privacy.
Transparency: Maintain transparency regarding automated processes and the handling of sensitive data.
Authorization: Ensure that appropriate authorizations are in place for automated actions, particularly those involving system changes.

Automating incident response processes using Python enhances the efficiency and effectiveness of cybersecurity operations. By leveraging automation for incident detection, triage, response, and reporting, organizations can respond to threats more swiftly and consistently. Python serves as a versatile tool for implementing these automated processes, allowing for customization and integration with existing security tools. However, ethical considerations must guide all automation efforts to ensure responsible practices in managing security incidents. As the threat landscape continues to evolve, mastering incident response automation will be essential for maintaining robust cybersecurity defenses.

Chapter 17: Future Trends in Network Security with Python and Scapy

Introduction to Future Trends in Network Security

The field of network security is constantly evolving in response to emerging threats, technological advancements, and changing regulatory landscapes. As organizations strive to protect their assets and data, they must adapt their security practices accordingly. This chapter explores the future trends in network security, particularly focusing on how Python and Scapy can be leveraged to address these trends effectively.

The Evolving Threat Landscape

As technology advances, so do the tactics employed by cybercriminals. The future of network security will be shaped by several key trends in the threat landscape:

Increased Use of AI and Machine Learning: Attackers are increasingly leveraging artificial intelligence (AI) and machine learning (ML) to automate attacks, making them more sophisticated and harder to detect.

Rise of IoT Vulnerabilities: The proliferation of Internet of Things (IoT) devices introduces new vulnerabilities, as many of these devices lack robust security features.

Cloud Security Challenges: As organizations migrate to cloud-based solutions, the security of cloud environments becomes a critical concern. Misconfigurations and inadequate access controls are common issues.

Remote Work Security: The shift towards remote work has created new attack vectors, as employees access corporate networks from unsecured locations and devices.

Leveraging Python for Network Security

Python is an invaluable tool in network security, offering flexibility and a vast array of libraries for various security tasks. Here are some ways Python can be utilized to address future trends:

AI and Machine Learning for Threat Detection

Python's extensive machine learning libraries, such as Scikit-learn and TensorFlow, can be employed to develop models that predict and detect anomalies in network traffic.

Example: Anomaly Detection Using Machine Learning

A Python script can be used to analyze network traffic patterns and detect anomalies indicative of potential threats.

python
Copy code
```
from sklearn.ensemble import IsolationForest
import pandas as pd

# Load network traffic data
data = pd.read_csv("network_traffic.csv")

# Prepare data for modeling
X = data[['packet_size', 'protocol', 'source_ip']]

# Train an Isolation Forest model for anomaly detection
model = IsolationForest(contamination=0.05)
model.fit(X)
```

```python
# Predict anomalies
data['anomaly'] = model.predict(X)
print(data[data['anomaly'] == -1])   #
Anomalies will be marked as -1
```

This script employs an Isolation Forest model to identify anomalous traffic patterns, enabling proactive threat detection.

Securing IoT Devices

As IoT devices become ubiquitous, ensuring their security is paramount. Python can be used to develop security frameworks for IoT ecosystems, including monitoring and management tools.

Example: Monitoring IoT Device Security

You can use Python to create a monitoring system that checks for vulnerabilities in connected IoT devices.

python
Copy code
```python
import requests

def check_device_security(device_ip):
```

```
response                            =
requests.get(f"http://{device_ip}/secu
rity_status")
return response.json()

# Example usage
device_ips      =       ["192.168.1.10",
"192.168.1.11"]
for ip in device_ips:
status = check_device_security(ip)
print(f"Security    status    for    {ip}:
{status}")
```

This script checks the security status of IoT devices, enabling quick identification of vulnerabilities.

Enhancing Cloud Security

Cloud security tools built with Python can help organizations monitor their cloud environments for misconfigurations and vulnerabilities.

Example: Checking for Cloud Misconfigurations

You can create a Python script that audits cloud configurations and alerts on potential security issues.

python
Copy code
```python
import boto3

def audit_s3_buckets():
s3 = boto3.client('s3')
buckets = s3.list_buckets()['Buckets']

for bucket in buckets:
acl                           =
s3.get_bucket_acl(Bucket=bucket['Name'
])
if any(grant['Permission']  ==  'READ'
for grant in acl['Grants']):
print(f"Bucket   {bucket['Name']}   has
public read access.")

# Example usage
audit_s3_buckets()
```

This script checks AWS S3 buckets for public read access, a common misconfiguration.

Remote Work Security Solutions

As remote work becomes the norm, Python can be utilized to develop solutions that secure remote access to corporate networks.

Example: VPN Connection Monitoring

A Python script can be created to monitor VPN connections and ensure that they are secure.

python
Copy code
```python
import psutil

def monitor_vpn_connections():
for                 conn                 in
psutil.net_connections(kind='tcp'):
if "VPN" in conn.laddr:
print(f"Active         VPN         connection:
{conn.laddr}")

# Example usage
monitor_vpn_connections()
```

This script monitors active TCP connections, identifying secure VPN connections.

Emerging Technologies and Python's Role

The future of network security will also be influenced by emerging technologies. Here are a few notable ones:

Zero Trust Architecture

The Zero Trust model emphasizes never trusting any device or user by default. Python can help automate the implementation of Zero Trust principles by verifying user identities and monitoring access.

Blockchain for Security

Blockchain technology can enhance security through decentralization and transparency. Python can be used to develop blockchain-based solutions for secure data sharing and transaction verification.

Quantum Computing Implications

The advent of quantum computing poses challenges to traditional encryption methods. Python can be utilized to explore quantum-resistant algorithms and develop quantum-safe security measures.

Community and Collaboration

The future of network security will increasingly rely on community collaboration. Open-source tools and frameworks developed in Python can facilitate information sharing and collective defense against cyber threats.

Contribution to Open Source Projects

Security professionals can contribute to open-source projects in Python, enhancing the community's ability to respond to threats.

Knowledge Sharing

Platforms for sharing knowledge and best practices in network security will grow in importance. Python-based educational resources can help train the next generation of security professionals.

Ethical Considerations in Network Security

As the field of network security evolves, ethical considerations will remain paramount:

Data Privacy: Ensuring that security measures do not infringe on user privacy rights is critical.

Responsible Disclosure: Security researchers must adhere to responsible disclosure practices when identifying vulnerabilities.

Inclusivity: Promoting inclusivity in security practices ensures that solutions are accessible to all organizations, regardless of size or resources.

The future of network security is poised for significant transformation, driven by emerging technologies and evolving threats. Python and Scapy will continue to play vital roles in developing innovative security solutions that address these challenges. By leveraging automation, machine learning, and community collaboration, organizations can enhance their security posture and effectively respond to threats. As we navigate this dynamic landscape, ethical considerations will guide our efforts to create a safer digital environment for all.

www.ingramcontent.com/pod-product-compliance
Lightning Source LLC
LaVergne TN
LVHW051336050326
832903LV00031B/3573